From Corporate to Country

Walking Away From a Career to Follow a Dream

Suzanne Gomes

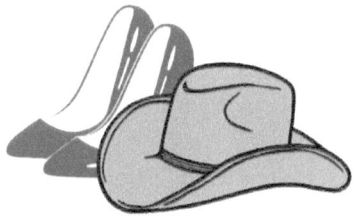

This book is dedicated to my parents, Noel and Pat.

Your love, support and encouragement throughout my life has enabled me to become the woman I am today. Thank you for always being my cheer squad.

I will always make you proud of ME!

First published by Ultimate World Publishing 2022
Copyright © 2022 Suzanne Gomes

ISBN

Paperback: 978-1-922828-14-9
Ebook: 978-1-922828-15-6

Suzanne Gomes has asserted her rights under the Copyright, Designs and Patents Act 1988 to be identified as the author of this work. The information in this book is based on the author's experiences and opinions. The publisher specifically disclaims responsibility for any adverse consequences which may result from use of the information contained herein. Permission to use information has been sought by the author. Any breaches will be rectified in further editions of the book.

All rights reserved. No part of this publication may be reproduced, stored in or introduced into a retrieval system, or transmitted in any form, or by any means (electronic, mechanical, photocopying, recording or otherwise) without the prior written permission of the author. Any person who does any unauthorised act in relation to this publication may be liable to criminal prosecution and civil claims for damages. Enquiries should be made through the publisher.

Cover design: Ultimate World Publishing
Layout and typesetting: Ultimate World Publishing
Editor: Isabelle Russell

Ultimate World Publishing
Diamond Creek,
Victoria Australia 3089
www.writeabook.com.au

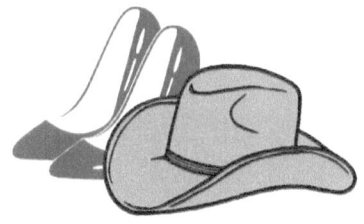

Contents

Introduction	1
Chapter 1: Corporate Life Begins	5
Chapter 2: First Taste of Management	11
Chapter 3: Authentic Leadership	25
Chapter 4: Middle Management	43
Chapter 5: One Chick, Many Men	67
Chapter 6: The Boys' Club	79
Chapter 7: Losing the Passion	95
Chapter 8: A Country Girl at Heart	103
Chapter 9: Living the Country Life Alone	115
Chapter 10: The Power of Animals	129
Chapter 11: Getting Down and Dirty	151
Chapter 12: Creatures Great and Small	171
Chapter 13: Preparation for the Cabins Begins	181
Chapter 14: Feeling Trapped	195
Chapter 15: Finding Me	207
Acknowledgements	217
About the Author	221
From Corporate to Country Bonus Offer	223

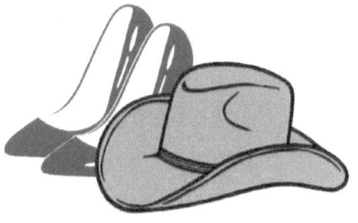

Introduction

'What do you want to be when you grow up, Suzanne?'

'Maybe a policewoman or a flight attendant!'

This is my earliest memory of what I was going to grow up to be. I never thought about being an inspiration to others, or being courageous, brave, or happy. When we were children and we got asked this question, we always referred to a job.

Years later, when I was in my last year of high school, the question was raised again, although now it had a serious tone: 'What do you want to be when you leave school, Suzanne?' A physical education teacher, maybe a policewoman, I thought. The questions always continued down the same route: 'What profession are you going to go into as a job?'

I was never asked what my values were or what I was passionate about.

When I left school, I went into nursing, which I had never even thought about previously. It was the course that I could get into as my grades weren't that good. But I embraced it as it was my first choice. I thought, 'I will look after people, I will help them recover.' It was a needs-based job that people would be thankful for.

After 18 months of nursing, I had an awfully bad bout of tonsilitis that saw me take quite some time off university and I had to defer. My parents would ask me, 'When are you going to get a full-time job, Suzanne?' Working casually in a chicken takeaway shop was not going to cut it at home!

At the age of 20, I went and got myself a traineeship in administration. A far cry from the policewoman, the flight attendant, the physical education teacher and the nurse.

But it didn't matter what I did, as long as I did something. If I had a job, I would bring in my own money, I wouldn't rely on my parents and they would be happy.

For many years, my dreams of having a purposeful career were gone. I wasn't going to graduate university – I wasn't going to be a nurse. I was going to be a personal assistant and for me at that time in my life was good. I enjoyed what I did, and I didn't really have any further aspirations. I was happy and had a regular income.

The administration traineeship went for nine months and after it finished, I was offered a permanent role with my employer, a government organisation financially supported by the councils in the western suburbs. There was just me and one other employee in the office, my boss, and we did administration tasks for the managers.

INTRODUCTION

Then, in 1994, I was made redundant. I don't remember being out of work for long before my dad told me they were advertising for call centre consultants at one of Australia's biggest companies. My father and many of my family had worked there for years. The money was good, better than where I had last worked, and my father had worked there for 38 years, so there would be longevity.

This is what started a 25-year career. Never in my wildest dreams did I believe that I would work at one company for 25 years. Nor did I believe I would climb the corporate ladder and become an executive. Someone who would inspire others and be a role model to many.

This young woman who only just passed Year 12, who didn't graduate from university, was on a path that she had never even dreamed of. This young woman who had so much in front of her but who didn't know how to navigate an interview, much less a successful career, was about to make her family proud.

How did a 21-year-old woman turn into a corporate executive? How did she navigate the corporate world? How did she manage to learn the skills to lead large workforces and manage the politics of corporate life?

Following this, how did she make the decision to walk away from it all to live in the country? To turn her back on the security of one of the best places to work in Australia. To leave behind the big pay packet and the responsibility of a job that at one stage she loved.

How did I transition from a corporate life with so much ahead of me, to life in the country, to a life on 35 acres? A place to heal, a place of serenity, a place of solitude. A place that would mend her heart, open her heart and allow her to follow her heart to fulfil her dream!

From Corporate to Country is all of that and more.

I will take you on an adventure that I never dreamed was possible. I will take you through the tough times and the amazing times. I will give you a look at the heartache, the resilience and the strength it has taken to manoeuvre between the two lifestyles, and how full my heart has become.

I always had a dream of a life in the country. A life that was gifted to me from the man that stole my heart and loved me for many years. He gifted me a story, a story to be told, to be listened to and hopefully to inspire. Inspire the people who say, 'I can never do that. I don't have the courage.'

I didn't think I could do it either. But when your dream and passion are so strong, you can do anything!

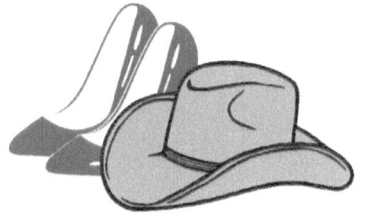

Chapter 1

Corporate Life Begins

In November 1994, I started working as a call centre consultant in an office in Footscray, Melbourne. The first day walking into the training room with a group of 20 was daunting. But it didn't take long to be trained, become competent and start to hit my numbers.

The team environment within the office was pretty good and my first supervisor was OK. He kept to himself and if we hit our calls per day then everything was great. We were able to do overtime at night and sometimes on Saturdays, which gave me some extra money when I wanted it.

After my first year at the call centre, I was asked to do relief for a specific role that wasn't on calls full-time. I liked taking up these opportunities as being yelled at, a few times a day because people couldn't pay their bills, wasn't fun. I filled in for others on a regular basis in these off-call positions, and started to build up my skills and knowledge.

During 1996, I was asked to join the specialist team full-time in a project management role. Managing jobs that were at risk of not meeting deadlines. I would have to liaise with customers, but also with the field area to ensure we could meet the work on time. I liked the role, and it wasn't long before my next opportunity was presented to me.

In February 1997, after three people had knocked back a role to work on the field side of the project management role, I was asked to go over for three to six months. I wasn't there as the first choice, but why not. It was at this point that I realised that if I was going to earn more money with more skills, then I would just say yes to new roles, whether I knew how to do them or not. If someone wanted me to do something else, then why not – especially if it was at a higher wage.

Off I went and started working in the field depot. This was a smaller team, with around 15 people working on the floor. The manager of the team was great, the officer in charge was not only great to work with, but also pretty good looking and there was lots of laughter.

As with most companies, in August 1997, there was a restructure and all the small field offices were amalgamated into one larger office. I was asked to apply for the permanent role that would be positioned on the other side of the city, an hour's drive from home. My supervisor, Robert, who was now a friend, was asked to apply as well. Together we made a great team and after a chat, which was referred to as an interview, we won the roles and got a very good pay rise.

Because of the drive that we would need to do each day, we asked our new supervisor if Robert and I could have the same shift so we could drive together. They were very accommodating and agreed wholeheartedly. We came with very good skills and knowledge and at that point, they just wanted us to be part of the team.

CORPORATE LIFE BEGINS

I still remember the first day we drove over to Moorabbin. We didn't know anyone, and Robert was quite a friendly guy, so he kicked it off with the new staff straight away. Me, I was a little bit more reserved back then and ended up getting a migraine halfway through the day. I didn't want anyone to know I had it, so as my sight went blurry and I could hardly see the screens, I took a few Panadol and persevered.

After getting home and nursing a bad headache, I really didn't want to go the next day. It was new, with new people, but Robert was driving me and I had at least one friend there. I worked through my fears and anxieties and settled into the team quite quickly.

It didn't take long for Robert to be asked to be a team leader within the centre. Before Christmas 1997, they moved to a new office in Springvale, amalgamating with another team. The dispatch centre, with its extended team, started to work together and I found them to be a good group of people.

It was also around this time that I started to fall for Robert. He had a girlfriend at that stage, and I had a boyfriend, but things weren't great on my side. Spending so much time with Robert in the car for over two hours a day, at work and sometimes having lunch together, I found him to be a super fun guy and a great person to be around. We also barracked for the same football team and I had started to go to games on Friday nights after work with him and his mate.

Love didn't blossom immediately. I was very professional at work and, to be honest, Robert wasn't giving me any cues that he was interested. I gave hints, but he never got them. He thought I was just being nice to him as a friend and even the bottle of scotch for Christmas in 1997 didn't get a reaction!

In 1998, I took on a couple of more specialist roles in the centre. They were more to do with planning the work and making sure we had enough staff in the field to do the work. It was a pretty good group, just six of us. It was still on the same floor as the dispatch team, but we felt a little more special.

1998 was also the year that Robert and I took the next step. We finally told each other we were interested in one another and wanted to give the relationship a go. It turned out most of our colleagues thought we were already together. We didn't really have to hide anything because most of them thought we were hiding our relationship anyway.

During that year, I took a two-week trip to Brisbane to undertake a planning training course that was rolled out to all planning roles nationally. I went with a colleague of mine and we really enjoyed meeting other colleagues from interstate and understand what they did. Robert also had the opportunity to undertake the course, and on both trips we each flew up to Brisbane to see each other and spent time on the Gold Coast.

What a job I had come into. It had only been three years since I joined the company. I had gone from a call centre consultant, and practically doubled my wage, to a planning specialist. I had attended several training courses and been flown interstate, all expenses paid. I couldn't have been happier, and I worked hard to achieve my performance metrics and get the best results I could.

At this time, I never remember thinking I was anything special at work. I did my job to the best of my ability. At times I would get frustrated, but nothing that was over the top. I was now 25, still living at home, and my parents were proud of what I was doing. Plus, the overtime was helping me to save a deposit on a unit. However, I never ended up purchasing that unit – instead, I used half the money to go on a five-week

CORPORATE LIFE BEGINS

holiday in November 1998 with Robert. We went to London, Paris, drove around the United Kingdom and Scotland and then ended up in Bangkok for some hot weather before returning home for Christmas.

It was also in Paris where Robert proposed to me up the Eiffel Tower. What a romantic. He got down on his knee and asked me to marry him. I was so in love with him and didn't want to ever be with anyone else. I said yes and we couldn't have been happier.

When we returned to work, with an engagement ring on my finger and smiles from ear to ear, no one was surprised, but all were so happy for us. They put a cake on for us and gave us their wishes.

Work didn't change much during 1999. I remember doing the same planning role and a few relief roles. At one point I ended up working for Robert back in the dispatch centre as they had centralised the planning roles to another state. Working for Robert annoyed me at times, as he would ask me to do tasks that others wouldn't and I always seemed to be working harder than anyone else in the team.

Before we got married in November 1999, Robert and I bought a house. At the start of 2000, I remember doing a lot of overtime in preparation for the move into our new home. Earning great money was what motivated me to get out of bed to be at work at 5:30 am and not get home until 7 pm some nights.

In 2001, I was asked to go for a role back in the field again. A specialist role which would support the team managers in the field – one where Robert and I would then be working in different offices and one that would give me another set of skills for the future.

I moved into the office in Collins Street in the city. The team, position and manager were all new. I hadn't worked with any of these team managers before, much less my manager. The other women in the office were nice to work with, the biggest factor was I was in the city and could go shopping on my lunch breaks. Woohoo!

This role was going to be my taste of real management. So far, my career and the roles I had undertaken had given me great skills and knowledge. All the managers that I had worked for always had good things to say about me. Now was my opportunity to step up and really shine.

One of my favourite parts of my job was meeting the employees in the field

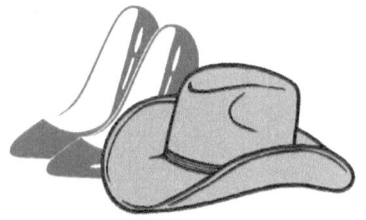

Chapter 2

First Taste of Management

In 2001, after moving into the specialist role in the city, I worked for a manager who saw a lot of potential in me. My role involved undertaking data analytics on the field and reporting out to the team managers in our area. I was working with them to fix performance, improve safety and resolve customer complaints.

My manager always had an open-door policy and he made sure I was given an equal voice in our team. But what I enjoyed most of all was that he took the opportunity to mentor me. He would coach me on different leadership skills, and because I really liked his style and his approach, he was the first manager that I had a lot of time and respect for.

He was also the first manager that I undertook relief for. He trusted and believed in me so much that he was happy for me to sit in his role while he took leave.

At this time in my working life, I knew I did my job well, that I was well liked and respected and we always achieved good results in our team. But to have me step into his role, this role that typically was undertaken by men, certainly not by a 28-year-old woman, he took a huge chance on me.

In the week leading up to his relief, he showed me the ropes, I sat in on several meetings with him and on the Friday, he handed the reins over to me. I was so nervous and, on the Monday, when I arrived in the office, I said hello to his personal assistant, who I already knew, and opened his email. I was elated but scared. It felt foreign to me and I really didn't know what the next three weeks would hold.

My fears were realised in the second week. Sitting in his role was a disaster that, it turned out, would rock me to the core and at the time I didn't think I would ever have the confidence to be in a management role again.

On the morning of the second Monday, I was notified that the team and I would be undertaking a safety audit. The process of the safety audit was that you are notified 24 hours before the audit started. You would then pick a team of individuals who would be interviewed both in the office and field and they would review the individual and team practices to make sure they were in line with the processes we were legally required to follow.

That afternoon, I met up with the team and put the interviews in place for the next few days. On the morning of day one, the auditing team, an external team in the depot, arrived. They briefed us on the process before interviewing me and several of the team managers and specialists.

I had to produce the documents that proved we had the procedures in place. We had to show evidence that we were monitoring them regularly, which they would then conduct audits in the field to observe that the practices were working.

I was nervous. I had participated in these audits before being a member of the team, as we had to conduct these internally at least once a year. But to be interviewed as manager was on a different level. The auditing team was good to me, and the interview went as well as I could perform it.

When they went into the field on day two of the three-day audit, everything fell apart. The auditors started to find illegal equipment. Makeshift tools that if used around electricity could kill someone if not themselves. Some of the vehicles had storage issues – their vehicles were a mess, just a mountain of unacceptable issues. By the end of day two the audit was stopped and deemed that there was too much that wasn't being followed correctly that they had to cease it.

This had never happened before. I took it on that it reflected me and that the team was not conducting the correct auditing techniques to keep our people and customers safe. As a result, the National Health and Safety manager was put on a flight at 2 pm and arrived from Sydney to address the team. At 4 pm, he sat us all down and gave us the worst speech I could have ever heard.

He yelled at us and called us the most appalling names. We couldn't defend ourselves against any of his accusations, and I must say some of it was undefendable. It was embarrassing. My heart was racing, my stomach turning, and sitting at the end of the table listening to the comments he was making about us brought tears to my eyes. Look, I knew that this was unacceptable, but the abuse he gave us once the auditors left the room was beyond unacceptable. I had never been spoken to or belittled like this in my career so far.

All I could do was cry. I was being made accountable for everything that was seen. He didn't care if I was in the chair for two minutes or 20 years – I was part of this team and we had to be made accountable.

I felt so alone. The team managers were making excuses that even I knew were unacceptable. I didn't know what to do, I had a headache that was pounding. I didn't know where to start, what to say, I was lost. I was lost in a world that I thought I didn't belong in.

Why did I accept this gig? Yes, it was only for three weeks, but seriously, I wondered, what was I doing? I was so far outside of my league that if this was what management is all about then I didn't want to be there. It was the worst day of my working life, and I felt like I just didn't belong.

The next day, I went to work, and first up after meeting with the team, the same national safety manager came in with the regional manager to talk to us about what we were going to do. They were giving us instructions; the national safety manager was being rude and abusive again. He had such an authoritarian, dictatorial style. No one in the room, probably most of the organisation, liked him or had any respect for him. Thankfully, the local safety team in our state were there and were trying to give me some reassurance of, 'This isn't your fault. Let's calm down, sit down and start to work on what's next.'

But it all got too much for me, and after crying in the toilet and office for what seemed like hours, after the health and safety sergeant told me, 'Someone's head will role after this,' I ran out of the office. I was so upset. I had my phone and rang Robert. I didn't want anyone in the team to see me because now I was acting like I wasn't capable to do the job. I couldn't even string a sentence together.

Back in the office, the team were worried, they didn't know where I was or what I was doing. They were worried for my safety and what

I could potentially do to myself. A few of the team managers knew it wasn't my fault. There were members of the team that had let the rest of us down. But I was the one that was leading this team and I had to deal with the consequences which, right now, I wasn't.

I walked to the nearest park with my sunglasses on, sat down on a bench and continued to cry. I wanted to find a rock and hide under it and never show my face to the team again.

The manager's assistant was so worried about me that she rang my manager who was on leave at the time and told him he had to come back immediately. I had already notified him what had happened. Not because I wanted him to return, but I knew he would want to know.

My manager came back to work that afternoon, and as I sat in the park alone, he walked up to me, sat down and gave me a hug. My head was hurting so much. I couldn't control my tears or talk, and all I could do was just cry and cry. He hugged me saying, 'It's OK, Suzanne, it's going to be OK. It's not your fault. I am taking full responsibility for this. We will work it out. The team and you and I, we will work through it. We will regain confidence and control in the field again.'

I couldn't rationalise anything at that stage – all I could do was cry. After about 30 minutes, he rang Robert, who picked me up and I went on sick leave for two days. But I wasn't a quitter.

The team were worried about me. My manager rang me both days and he came back to work the next day. I felt guilty that this guy had left his family to come back to work and I had to stand up.

On the Friday, I made the decision to return to work on the Monday. That the team and I would start making things right. We would put the plan together, we would start auditing every field member and we would address all the non-compliance and deliver disciplinary action where necessary.

This was the first time that I decided that if you're part of a team, you stand together with them. You work with them. You lead them out of the biggest shit-hole you have ever had to deal with and you gain their respect by not letting them down. Running to the park may have not been the most mature thing to do and I can't do it every time something went wrong. But it was a lesson to work out how to take stock, take a deep breath, raise your chin, and lead your team forward.

At first, I was embarrassed by the way I reacted, crying in front of the team, leaving them in the lurch, not being able to have the courage or resilience to stick with them. I learnt some very valuable lessons that allowed me to take on future leadership roles. It was the start of building who I wanted to be, that leadership was in my blood.

On Monday, the team joined me back in the office. They gave me an overview of the next steps. My manager went back on leave, and we got shit done. We worked so hard. I was out in the field with my managers, I was inspecting their work as well as the staff and we cleaned that mess up. It was a massive introduction to being a leader and one I will never forget.

This wouldn't be the first time that I would be dealt a harsh lesson or two. When you are leading large groups of people, the only way you learn is to have to encounter setbacks, have things go wrong or have people disappoint you.

FIRST TASTE OF MANAGEMENT

After a couple more stints in relief manager roles, I was then asked to move into the regional health and safety role. I am not sure if it was because of what had happened two years earlier, or it was really because the regional manager at the time saw potential and wanted to expand my skill set. If I was going to have a manager's role in the future, they wanted me to broaden my experience.

A few weeks into this role, and after the manager decided my colleague could take some time off, I had to assist with managing an accident that could have turned fatal.

A worker had fallen from a great height, which had been witnessed by a few people in the building, and I was asked to drive to the site to support the workers that had witnessed the event plus the team managers.

When I arrived, all I could see was blood. The ambulance had taken the worker to hospital as his colleagues had rung 000 immediately after the accident occurred. He had extensive head injuries and there was a full-blown incident investigation that needed to be managed.

I hadn't come across anything like this before. The team onsite set up roles for each of us. I was accountable for organising the employee assistance team to come on site and providing supportive assistance to the traumatised workers who had witnessed the event.

These workers had not only witnessed it, but each of them was being investigated to understand how someone could have suffered such a terrible fall. The guys that were there were crying, visibly upset. All I could think of doing was comforting them. I wanted them to know that we would support them and all they had to do was tell the truth. Tell the managers what they saw and if they remembered something later, because a couple of them were in shock, they were to write it down and tell us straight away.

It was such a terrible time for everyone on site. All I had to do was be calm and make sure everyone was doing OK. I made lots of cups of tea and handed out many bottles of water. The guys needed someone calm, so I took on that role.

The last thing I remember on that day was helping to clean up the blood after all the evidence and pictures were taken. The smears that were on the floor from the mop were confronting. We had cleaners coming in, but I just wanted to get it cleaned up immediately as I didn't want the guys who had witnessed the accident to see the remnants and cause them further heartache all over again.

I learnt a lesson that day – it doesn't matter what has happened to someone or something; at times like these, you need to bring compassion to the role. People don't do things to cause harm, but these guys were in shock and they needed us to be calm, present and willing to listen. To help them through one of the worst events that we had all witnessed.

Thankfully, the employee recovered, although he did suffer some level of brain damage and never returned to the field.

Two years later, we would meet again when I took on my first management role and had to medical retire him. He couldn't perform his pre-accident duties and I helped his wife and him to secure a payout via his superannuation that allowed him to continue to have a reasonable quality of life.

It was hard on them, but I was glad that I ended up being the one that helped them secure the financial security that, hopefully, would allow him to live a better life.

As a leader, I also had to visit many employees' homes. In 2005 I visited an employee that needed a liver transplant. He was on the transplant list and as I sat opposite him and his wife, drinking a cup of tea and watching how sick he was, it was heartening that he was able to spend an hour with me, while I told them both we would support them now and post-transplant.

Unfortunately, two weeks later, he didn't receive his transplant in time, and he died. I then had the heartbreaking task of going to see his wife to support her and give our condolences. I felt grateful to walk away knowing that I worked for a company that was compassionate about what a family needs. I knew I had to ease the wife's pain by helping her get through her husband's work documents. We would help to lessen her burden so she had one less thing to worry about while dealing with her husband's death.

When an employee died, making that initial visit always made me feel sick until the family opened the front door. I think being a woman gave me a level of empathy and care that made families feel at ease in my presence. I really felt for these families, and it was very rewarding that I could help them in their time of grief.

I had to visit customers on my own at times, as I was sometimes the highest executive in the state, and I was accountable for the nation's customer service.

I remember going to Bundaberg four times in 2013 after the floods and meeting with a businessman who owned a motel that had been flooded four times in just three years. He had lost everything, repeatedly. As he stood in front of me, telling his story of loss, he broke down and started to cry. It was heartbreaking to see this man so helpless and empty. I couldn't stand there and do nothing, so I went over to him and gave him a hug. I didn't care if it was inappropriate or not, I just had this overwhelming feeling to support him.

After talking to him some more and offering a few things to help him out, it was hard to turn away and say goodbye. We couldn't give him his business back, but he was so appreciative that we had come out to see him, that we had comforted him and that we cared.

I was asked on several occasions to ring customers whose partner had died, and although the company wasn't at fault, if we didn't have their service running or our infrastructure had contributed, then it was the executive's role to be the contact. I remember talking to one man in Melbourne, where his wife had fallen over in the street and hit her head. No one was around to witness it, but our infrastructure was alleged to have contributed.

He was such a lovely man. I would call him every couple of weeks, or he would call me to discuss any questions that he may have had. Just being able to have a direct contact that could help him work through the possible liability eased his mind. He even apologised to me one day as his daughter had rung and abused me. I told him that was OK, that she was in a lot of pain and that I had empathy for their situation. He thanked me profusely and wrote a letter to our human resources department stating how grateful he was for what I was able to do for them.

During storms, our customers would sometimes be affected by outages, especially during lightning storms. Due to the rocky terrain that some customers lived around, it would sometimes happen every year.

A customer on the border of Queensland and New South Wales had this issue. He was in his seventies and after I went into the executive role and it had happened once, I gave him my number and he could call me direct whenever it happened.

It didn't matter where we shifted the infrastructure, every year during extreme electrical storms in October/November, lightning would strike. Then I would be abused for not putting it in the right spot. With certain customers, I just sat on the phone and listened – and he was one of them. I would organise our crews to go out to put temporary infrastructure in place, then permanent after the rains stopped. But nothing we did was what he wanted and what he wanted was impossible to do.

I hadn't heard from him for a while, until one day when I received a call from his daughter. She rang me up to tell me her dad had died, that I wouldn't be hearing from him and that they were going to sell his property. The reason she called me was to apologise for the way her father had yelled at my staff and I for so many years. She said she felt sorry for what he had said and that she wanted me to know that.

I couldn't believe that she had done that. But sometimes, there were customers who, even though you knew you were doing everything you could to resolve their issues, still yelled abuse at you. You could spend days on one customer's projects and most of the time they were pleasant and thankful for the work that we did. But there were a handful of customers that had my number that I would always take a breath before answering as I knew what would come next!

In 2013, we had a customer whose partner was in hospital and after a bad storm in the back parts of Brisbane their service had gone out. The area they lived in was beautiful but hilly, and they lived in a gully full of trees. Unfortunately, their service wasn't working after the infrastructure was taken down by a fallen tree and the hospital hadn't been able to call her.

When she went up to ring the hospital, she found out that her partner had died during the night. Unfortunately, the hospital had written down the wrong mobile number for her and they hadn't been able to get her on that either.

As a result of what had happened, I went and visited the lady to offer my condolences. To get to their house in the gully, you needed a four-wheel drive and then to walk up a steep embankment to the house. I met with her a couple of times to not only resolve the infrastructure issue, but as I learned that she was in financial hardship, I helped her with a payment plan for her bills. This gave her some relief and she was very appreciative.

I liaised with her for a month or so, and after a while, I became the main contact for any issues the community had. I would sometimes go out and see the customers and talk to them about opportunities to help them with their communications and they were all genuinely nice people. I didn't expect for the community of 10 houses to all have my number, but it was rewarding to help them out when I could.

I encountered so many different challenges that I had never experienced before. There were always lessons to be learnt, there were times of failure, and once I got into my executive years, I started to gain more confidence with my team to try things. Give it a go, dive into the unknown and learn, learn, learn. Resilience is built through challenging times. As the saying goes, 'You never know how strong you are until being strong is the only choice you have.'

My Lesson for You:

- It takes three to five months to get comfortable with and adjust to a new job.
- Challenges are lessons. Your biggest learnings will come from the hardest days or events.
- If you're not 100 per cent sure if you can deliver a 'yes', say 'no'. 'No' is better than 'maybe' or 'yes'. You can change 'no' to a 'yes' later if your circumstances change.
- When bad events happen, give yourself some time out, take a deep breath and make sure you are in control of yourself before you help others.
- Don't jump to conclusions about who or what is to blame. Always work through the what, why, when and who of any situation. Investigate thoroughly, put the action plan in place and address the gaps.
- Have genuine empathy for others.
- Have a friend or family member to talk to during hard times.

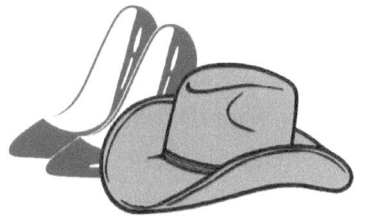

Chapter 3

Authentic Leadership

During my career, I quickly worked out how I wanted to lead my teams. I knew by taking on a leadership role you instantly become a role model, so when I saw my people doing the wrong thing, it was usually a reflection of me, which I had to identify and change quickly. But I also wanted my teams to be inclusive, creative and to have fun.

I always seemed to be able to build a good rapport with my people. I wanted everyone to feel that they had a voice at the table. If I saw, they weren't contributing I would then talk to them one on one. I wanted people to be creative. To give things a go through assessing any risks, implement it and share the results with others.

I loved being with my people. I spent a lot of time out with my teams, whether it was in the field visiting customers with them, working with them to learn how they did their jobs for a day, attending team meetings or sitting in call centres. Whatever it was that allowed me to understand my people, what they did and how I could help, I was out there doing it.

It did mean being away a lot. I spent a lot of time on the road, driving up to 1,500 kilometres in a week. There were a lot of early mornings and late nights. There was a lot of time spent on planes and in hotel rooms catching up on emails and other administration. But when I was away, I made the most of it. It was always double the workload, not managing days of emails, but it was what I loved.

I loved sharing the company and business strategy. I liked debating the issues and having my team implement solutions. I couldn't always give them 'yes' as an answer. But as a leader, I knew that if it was an answer that had to be given from me than I would do it. My philosophy was simple: if the answer was 'maybe', I would say 'no'. You can always change a 'no' to a 'yes'. But answering 'yes' or 'maybe' to a 'no' just disconnects people.

I loved celebrating employees' milestones. I would travel the country, presenting 50- and even 60-year service awards to employees that had been working longer than I had been alive. I loved meeting their families, taking them out to dinner and making sure they knew that I valued their commitment and work and so did the company.

The best trip I had was visiting an employee in Normanton, Queensland, where we only had two staff in the town. My flight landed in the morning and the manager and I met with the team leader.

Before we headed out of town to meet up with the employee, we needed to get fuel. The owner of the petrol station said to the team manager, 'I hear the big boss is in town.' The team leader responded, 'Yes, she is in the front seat if you want to meet her.' The attendee gave me an embarrassed look and walked inside. What amazed me was that everyone knew I was coming to celebrate the 40th work anniversary of a very respected member of the community.

That night, we had dinner at the employee's favourite establishment. The bar staff were amazing and they couldn't believe I had come all that way to celebrate their mate's achievement. They were so impressed that they opened early to make us the best country style hot breakfast that I have ever had. I was so appreciative of their response to me. This was what being away from my hubby for long periods was all about.

During the day, we went out and helped our employee finish an important job at the local school. He was impressed with my work ethic and we had some great chats. He then gave me a history lesson on the Burke and Wills track and told me I had to visit before leaving. When he shook my hand to say thank you and goodbye, I sensed genuine gratitude towards me. I gave him a hug, visited the Burke and Wills site and I will never forget my trip to Normanton.

During my time leading the field in Queensland and New South Wales, we introduced a leadership program that predominately focused on the leadership of the leader – improving the way they led meetings with their people, working through issues and improving processes, enhancing their one-on-one conversations and cascading information to their teams.

It was a valuable system and process. Some leaders didn't like it, as they were traditional authoritarian managers. They didn't like to be asked to change, to be more inclusive, calm, open and caring. They felt that there was no benefit to our approach and, at times, hated the weekly catch ups with their dedicated coach.

But it wasn't the case for most. You had leaders who couldn't get enough of the program. They believed in what the objectives were, they worked with their coach with ease and found that their jobs and the pressure they had doing their job was decreasing. The biggest bonus, which was the true objective of the program, was that they had more engaged teams.

With any change, you must make a conscious decision to stop certain practices in order to take up new ones. You can't do them all as that would've increased their stress levels. Each manager would roll out the process to each team manager and their employees. It took us nearly two years to completely role it out to everyone. But what I was seeing from the leaders that embraced it was happier more productive employees.

In 2018, the company put a top-down, from-the-CEO, five-day intensive leadership course in place for general managers and above. Throughout the five days, we were coached on problem solving in teams and working together in roleplay scenarios in which we assumed different roles. We had hard conversations about performance and worked on ourselves as leaders and in being authentic to our people. There was a lot more involved, but I truly believed that it was something that could have a positive impact on the culture and change the way our people viewed us.

Taking all the top-line managers out of the business for five days was a big investment. It was a time to step back, look within and identify what we needed to change in a safe environment where you could be honest without criticism. Some of the sessions were hard, and it got emotional, but overall it was so valuable for me.

I wanted to make sure that when my managers attended, they came back to work with a commitment of implementing their promises. We would monitor them through our one-on-one sessions and it made us more transparent leaders.

What I noticed around the company was that the implementation for ourselves and our people was not consistent across all business units. It was so disappointing when I heard others saying nothing has changed, nothing will change and it's not getting the right outcomes.

I was so committed that I put my hand up to be a mentor at one of the workshops. I took another week out of my role, which I had to balance both and supported the group that I was part of. Some of the confidential conversations I had with others about their ability to be a people manager or what was going on outside of work was confronting. But I was so determined to support these managers, not only at the workshop, but also outside of it.

I did have a couple of general managers contact me after that week for further support with implementing their actions. It was amazing to see several of them grow to one day achieve the next level or step in their career.

I know some of the managers are still using the tools and approach that they learnt back in 2011 and 2018. But others really struggled and as soon as I moved on from the leadership role, they stopped using it, which was a shame.

I always took what I had learnt from those programs into my next roles. It was a way of working that came naturally to me. It also wasn't all fluff. It did mean that you were having hard conversations and at times that was hard for some of my managers to hear.

For one of my managers, his approach and ability to adapt just didn't work out. He wouldn't be honest with me – his performance went down and he just couldn't get it together.

After putting a performance improvement plan in place, engaging an outside coach and lots of conversations, I had to meet with him face-to-face and give him the news that he wasn't capable to undertake the role.

It was a shock to him, even though we had been having hard conversations about his performance for three months. He couldn't see that his approach and him not adapting to this new way meant his team was the worst performing. Then, after working with him for a further three months, I had to end his position. He wasn't capable of being the people manager we needed, and although hard for him, it enabled me to put the right manager in his place.

Many of my managers would say that I was tough but fair. I saw some managers who would avoid the hard conversations and wouldn't be open about their performance. Our team unfortunately went through a period where we had to dismiss several employees. I made sure we did the due diligence, engaged human resources and went through the right process prior to dismissal to ensure it was fair.

We had employees who were dismissed for fraud, stealing, misconduct with customers, misconduct with managers, alcohol or drug use. Losing their licence, going home halfway through the day – the list went on. Every dismissal was not only hard for the employee but also for the managers. Some of the managers were close to these employees, but people make bad decisions and although everyone knew the rules in our business, some employees, for whatever reason, and we had a lot of those, just couldn't work within those parameters.

It was also hard for my managers to go through redundancy processes. Our business was changing on a regular basis. We communicated that the workloads were decreasing and, in some areas, significantly. We unfortunately would go through this process every year due to new enhancements in technology, new tools or new computer programs. But we all had to do it and it was part of our job.

In 2013, we had a major company restructure. It was one of the first times where our boss asked us to sort ourselves into groups of four to create and deliver a presentation of what a new structure could look like. The colleague I was working with had only been with the company a few years and the other one was undertaking a relief executive role. Both, like me, had seen the faults and opportunities this presented. With courage, we presented a structure that went from four executives leading the field to just one.

After we presented some silly song and dance to break the ice, which didn't work, the room fell silent. The managers, my colleagues, who had been there for years rejected the structure and said it wouldn't work. But our strategy general manager loved it and we persuaded our boss that the only way we would reduce spending and deliver what the company needed was to do it.

Within two hours of presenting the structure and doing some more work on it with three other team members, our boss approved it to be fully developed and implemented.

I was given the role to lead this nationally. It was such a privilege to be able to take on this role, but it also meant that I had a lot of change to introduce. My previous three colleagues had been in the business for several years and it was hard for them to go through this.

The day we announced the major restructure I was on leave but came into the office. My husband had been diagnosed with leukaemia two weeks prior and I had been by his bedside while he lay in hospital receiving chemotherapy. But I needed to announce the restructure, I was accountable for this change, so I came into work, specifically to role the new structure out.

My team who had been working on it with me also helped and supported me through the 50-page pack that we had to roll out. When I walked into the office, the first time that anyone had seen me since Robert's diagnosis, there were lots of condolences, hugs and asking how I was.

When we got the team on the call, it was straight down to business. At the end of the call I openly talked about Robert's diagnosis, that I had another week off caring for him, then I would return to work, to manage this piece and the team whilst still caring for my husband.

My days at work changed to 7:30 am to 3 pm. Every day, I would leave between 3 to 4 pm to visit Robert in hospital. It was a fine balance to manage them both, but with my parents arriving from Melbourne to help me out, it worked.

When I returned to work, the first task was to reduce the number of field managers through the redundancy process. I had 30 managers whom I had to reduce to just 22. A few of them elected to be made redundant, but it still meant I had to follow the process. Eight weeks into my husband's diagnosis, while he was undergoing his third round of chemotherapy, I was ringing managers telling them they didn't have a job.

During this time, a lot of my energy was being put into Robert's fight to live, so picking up the phone, although it made my stomach turn on every call, was a little easier knowing that most of these people would find a new job. Yes, it was heartbreaking for people to lose their job. But if I lost Robert that would be even more heartbreaking. So, rationalising between the two situations was how I managed.

This period did take its toll on me, because I was managing work and Robert's health. I was exhausted, and at times stressed, but my strength as an individual and leader was building, and I wanted to be accountable for the hard decisions at work and not leave it to someone else. Doing this gained a lot of respect from everyone around me and I had a lot of people helping me with other parts of my job because of balancing my life.

Throughout Robert's 20 weeks of treatment, 17 of which he spent in hospital, I managed both. When Robert was taken to ICU, I took a week off until he was out of the woods. Over Christmas, I took the days off that Robert was home from hospital and I had several of my managers take on my responsibilities during this time. It was great to see them stand up for me and keep the team running. They needed to work together and reduce my anxiety levels, which is what great teams do!

After Robert went into remission, I finished the restructure, put together a new team and started to lead without the stress of juggling work and life. I did start to change some of my approach. I do believe I began to be a lot less tolerant of people who complained about what I saw were trivial things. I had watched my husband go through chemotherapy and nearly die whilst in ICU, so I didn't need to manage selfish individuals who believed they were owed something.

That included my team. I got quite frustrated when they weren't displaying the leadership traits that we had learnt to implement a few years ago. When performance was being managed, some leaders didn't have the same discipline to addressing misconduct and I didn't put up with anyone who didn't respect me or what I was doing to improve the workplace.

I knew these employees had worked under authoritarian managers for most of their working life and to ask someone to trust me that my approach would be different was hard. But the areas that needed the most focus needed my time and with Robert's support, now in remission, I started to travel again.

Instead of travelling around Queensland, my focus went to Victoria, South and West Australia and the Northern Territory. Weeklong trips to remote locations, that would see us visit four to five teams in a week. Many hours on the road, but it was also a chance to get to know a new bunch of leaders.

Most of the trips went well. I got to visit customers in the Barossa Valley, along the Murray River, the Southern Coast of Western Australia, Albany and the Margaret River and even across to the Tiwi Islands via helicopter off Darwin. I met a diverse group of people and had a bit of fun along the way.

During the middle of 2013, I was contacted by the Customer Service Management Association as my team had nominated me for Customer Service Leader of the Year for Queensland. I was so overwhelmed with gratitude. They had nominated me for the way I always took accountability for our customers, improved customer service processes and ensure our people could talk to our customers with ease.

The Association came out and undertook an interview with me. They really liked what I had done, the examples of great customer service and the initiatives we had put in place. I won the Queensland Award and was then a nomination for the national award. As Robert had just been diagnosed with leukaemia and the awards were in Melbourne, I couldn't go, so a couple of my team attended on my behalf.

I didn't win the national award, but I didn't care. It wasn't about the award; it was that my team recognised the work that I did. The care I took with our customers, even if they did abuse me at times and that I cared enough to improve processes to make it easier for our people.

During 2018, I took on a project within the business that was related to cultural change. I was the Indigenous cultural lead and with eight other general management leads, we developed an action plan to drive Indigenous cultural awareness throughout the company.

Many of the actions involved, celebrating Naidoc Week, ensuring we are working within the company's Reconciliation Action Plan to engage our Indigenous employees, tell their stories and ensure our recruitment processes involved engaging Indigenous groups outside of the company and recruiting more Indigenous employees.

These were just some of the actions of a large piece of work. I learnt so much about the Indigenous culture, plus because I was part of a broader team with portfolios such as carers, disability and LGBT, I learnt a lot about inclusion and diversity and how to embed that into my teams. I really enjoyed my time leading this group and am so much greater for it.

During my time as an executive, I had the opportunity to host or emcee several events on behalf of the company. The first one was the companies bi-annual leadership conference. In 2013, twelve months after being rewarded my first executive role I was asked by our Chief Operations Officer (COO) to emcee the leadership conference on one of the two days, as a full day event. I would open and close the event, open every session and create some fun for the audience.

I was nervous every time I thought about the event for weeks leading up to it. The night and morning before the big event, I was rehearsing my lines in front of the mirror. No one expected me to learn the lines off by heart, but it was important that I spoke with confidence.

After the initial nerves and kicking the event off, I led the agenda into morning tea and it started to be fun. Here I was, in front of 300 colleagues, looking out, leading and showing my full potential. The

COO was full of compliments and even the CEO congratulated me on leading the day. I had never been so happy for what I had achieved. I started in this company as a call centre consultant and 18 years later I was leading the company's biggest leadership event.

The hosting roles didn't stop there. I had the opportunity to open and emcee the Women's Business Awards on behalf of the company. An event that was held every year in every state, leading up to the national awards.

I hosted the awards three times in Perth and Adelaide. Standing up on behalf of the company, representing women executives, was such a privilege and again a lot of fun.

The best part was announcing the Overall State Award winner. I even had the gold card that I would open and get to announce into the microphone, 'And the winner is…' I had a beaming smile in all the photos taken on the stage with the winners. I was nearly as happy and surprised as they were.

During these events, I had the opportunity to meet some inspirational women who were the guest speakers at the events. Lisa Camplin-Warner, Olympic gold medallist, Stephanie Alexander, Australian cook and food writer and leading brain surgeon, Fiona Kerr. I hosted female politicians who attended and sat at the main table with me and all the nominated women that I met were all very inspirational. There were always interesting conversations to be had at every event.

It was such a privilege to be part of these awards.

Outside of these roles, I also attended or led several leadership conferences. Some I participated in, some would have me lead a session or I would hold two-day meetings with my direct team every three months. The time you put into them and after the events were extremely important. If I attended one that my team did not, I would communicate what was discussed or actions taken from it to the teams via start of week calls, emails and videos.

One of my everyday roles involved identifying new talent. In a business which at times had 2,500 people, I would meet various people of all ages, diverse backgrounds and different locations who were all so talented. People who had never thought of taking that next step, were the ones I put my time into, as they just needed a little bit of encouragement and confidence to believe in themselves and enable them to fly!

I mentored several people throughout my time with the company. Most showed they had a great willingness to try new ways of approaching challenges, but some didn't. When I mentored someone for the first time, I always told them that these sessions were about improving something they feel they need to work on. Working on them meant doing activities, conversations or new approaches outside of the sessions. If I felt that they weren't putting the conversations or actions in place between our sessions, I would politely outline to the participant that this wasn't working for them or me, give them the reason why and stop the mentoring sessions.

Mentoring isn't just about the time the mentee is taking out of their day to be mentored. It also was time I was taking out of my day, to coach them to be the best that they could be. So, I needed to feel it was worthwhile. I wanted to see that the individual was growing, they were learning new methods, they were building confidence and they would one day strive to achieve their goals. That was extremely satisfying for me when I saw this happen.

In 2010, I met a female in the field who was undertaking a relief team manager role. She had predominantly worked in data analysis and project management roles, but she wanted to try her hand at leadership. When I met her, she was so nervous. She didn't say much, but I knew from the start she had a passion that ran deep and she could go somewhere. Her manager also believed in her talent and I was happy to support him with her development.

Over the years, she started to come out of her shell, gain more confidence and took on the manager role that her previous manager occupied, which led her to work for me. We worked on her confidence, being able to have a voice in our meetings and allow her to provide insight that her colleagues didn't see. Through being with her people and coaching them that they hadn't seen in a manager before, she started to lift performance to a level that her region had never achieved. Her employee satisfaction results started to rise and her confidence shone.

Over a period of 10 years, I have seen her go from a relief team manager to a general manager. She has moved around the country taking on roles that needed her leadership and expertise. She has been on the road and visited some diverse places and developed her own team, her way.

She has mentored her own group of talent and has become an amazing leader. I am so proud of what she has done, how she achieved it and her ability to see that she needed a mentor to help her navigate the political stage. I loved every conversation we ever had, and I am still watching her grow today.

The company also had a sponsor program for woman. The general managers would have an executive sponsor for six months. We would meet up with them monthly and we would assist them and introduce them to new people. When roles in the business came up, we would nominate them for relief or permanent positions to support their careers. I got to know several women that had such amazing talent that I hope have gone on to do great things.

I have mentored many women who have since gone on to launch their own businesses, take on executive roles and become the strong women they always dreamed of. Each of these women – and men, too – knew what they wanted to achieve, which skills they needed to develop and improve and they made a commitment to themselves, that even when the days got tough and some things didn't work, they kept their end goal in mind.

It's an amazing feeling when you help people to live their dreams, and I still love hearing about their achievements today.

Over my time in leadership roles spanning 15 years, there always seem to be some sort of large issue, a team that I had to take on because of bad performance or hard restructures. It was hard but very rewarding work, and over time I would even gain the title of Mrs Fix-It!

The skills that I have acquired during those times, are skills I depend on today. I have learnt so much from every person who I have worked for, worked for me and worked beside me. From the customers to the VIPs, there is never a time where you don't learn something from someone. This is what will shape you and allow you to become an authentic leader.

My Lesson for You:

- Know your team by spending time with your employees and understanding what they do and what motivates them.
- Engage your employees to improve the business. If a process is broken, engage the team working on it to ask them to improve it. Enable your team members to instigate change for good.
- Always have time for one-on-one sessions with your team members – quarterly at a minimum. Everyone needs feedback to know how they are working and whether they are regularly meeting their goals.
- Identify top talent and mentor them. They will be your success points.
- Ask your employees to show you, not tell you. Showing you the results is real.
- Listen more than you speak.
- Ask lots of questions.
- Coach, coach, coach. Repeat, repeat, repeat. No one gets it the first time.

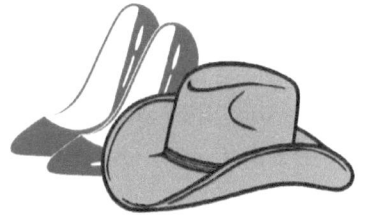

Chapter 4

Middle Management

After 12 months of undertaking a field manager role in Melbourne, where I lead a team of 12 team managers and 180 field staff, an opportunity came up for the Victorian operations manager role. It was a new role and would be a liaison for many functions and be the hub of the field operations supporting eight managers.

At this stage, it seemed the perfect role for me, and because I hadn't secured a role since my position was made redundant in 2003, I went for and won it.

In April 2006, after an eight-week holiday, I settled into the role, interviewing new direct reports and starting to liaise with my fellow operations managers in South Australia and Western Australia. There were also three other roles based in Queensland, New South Wales and Canberra and we all built a very good rapport and tried to be aligned via the same projects and objectives nationwide.

Most of the time, it was very challenging. The field managers that we all dealt with had big personalities. Our executive directors that we worked for had big personalities and the national groups that we also had to work with had their own objectives too.

Most of my role outside of driving initiatives was making sure we completed our workload every day and kept the boss happy by managing the politics. So many people thought that they had the answers to the gaps, blockers and issues. We would hold meetings and agree on a process, only to hear that someone had decided they didn't want to do it that way and implemented it their way.

The biggest issue that we had was when major weather events happened. During 2006-2008 it mostly seemed to be Queensland and we needed to move staff interstate to help them recover.

I distinctly remember there being a complete stuff-up by the Queensland acting director. He made a call, which was outside of the national call. I was told not to send staff his way that he didn't need them and they would cope on their own. As a result of many inquisitions of who said what to whom, he was asked to step down from his role.

But the bigger issue was the planning executive and the way he managed us when moving staff. He had an ego as big as the nation. He spoke to us like shit most of the time and it put our backs up every time he made a call that my boss and other executives wanted to question. Most of this time was managing phone calls, email and text messages back and forth, and when the wet season ended in Queensland it was a relief.

During this time, I also took the opportunity to continue to take on relief roles. I went into the dispatch centre for a month to help them manage the operational functions while their manager was offline planning a restructure. Most of the people that I managed were either previous team managers who managed me or colleagues.

Because the team's new restructure was underway, there were a lot of disgruntled employees. Some wouldn't undertake their roles the way they had been asked to and got quite angry.

One day, when I was sitting in the team manager pod, because I didn't sit in an office as I wanted to sit with the teams, one employee, a woman who I had worked with, got quite irate. I went over to her, asked her to calm down and stop disrupting the team. She continued to argue with me about what she believed was a better way of doing it. I told her the way she was talking to me was not the way to get her point across and I asked her to sit down. Again, she didn't, and she swore at me.

That was enough – my bubble had burst and I told her to either sit down or get out of my sight. She walked out still swearing and cursing. My blood was boiling, and for the first time, I felt out of control and shaking. One of the team managers told me I shouldn't have done what I did, so I told her that they should've addressed this behaviour months ago. It was out of line and she needed to respect the decisions we make.

An hour later, after another employee on the floor had started to argue and support this woman, she came back inside and we sat down with the team manager. By then, I was already prepared to issue her a written warning for her behaviour and I delivered the news to her. She wasn't happy, but we needed to deliver consequences to people who behaved like this. I had to deliver another written warning for similar behaviour a few weeks later to another employee from the same team.

The message got through to the 120 people on the floor. If you are not going to undertake the role in the way that we had trained you or behave disrespectfully towards others on the floor, there would be consequences. The managers in the workplace had not addressed the employees' concerns. There should've been ways in which the team could propose ideas and we would work through them. After this, I recommended that the team start this, which would help to engage the team and the centre. I don't know if they ever put my recommendations in place as I left the role a week later.

My time in that role taught me a lot about managing others who used to be your colleagues. At first, I was fearful about leading such people, but after I had led the team for a month and brought the behaviour into line, many of my old colleagues respected me for it.

Then, believe it or not, six months later, the woman I issued the written warning to came to work for me. At the end of the day, I knew she was smart with good intentions for what she wanted to drive in the business and she understood how the processes needed to be changed. So I knew she was the right person to be in my group to lead change.

Over the year or so that she worked for me, we got along well. I worked out how to get the best from her, she coached several new staff in the same role as her and we were the best performing region because of her work. When I was in the dispatch centre with her, she was clearly in the wrong job. It's amazing when you know you have talent and it's wasted on them. Put them in a different environment with a different manager and sometimes people shine.

In June 2008, after being in the operations manager role, undertaking a couple of relief field manager roles, I was asked to move into the business manager role. I was getting pretty used to being asked to step into different roles to help and of course it was increasing my knowledge of the business again.

Earlier that year, I had sat in for my boss, the director, so if I was ever going to have the opportunity to take on a general manager position or his role, I needed to learn the financial side of the business in more detail.

This was going to be quite a challenge for me. It was all about managing the business initiatives related to the finances, liaising with the financial manager and ensuring we met projected budgets.

I had done a bit of this when I was in the operations manager role, as I worked quite closely with the business manager. The business manager who was moving into another role, was a mate of mine, so I was confident enough to take on the role and have him support me.

The new systems and reports that I had to present took a bit of getting used to. Outside of work, I had taken on an accounting module at university around eight years ago, but I didn't remember much of it. I reminded myself that this was like managing our budget at home, just with a lot more zeroes! Only a budget of about $100 million.

I wasn't in the role for too long – I think I only presented two months of financials and was just getting my head around some of the tasks that I needed to deliver – when I was asked to take on another new role. The funny thing was, is that my boss had just taken off to Europe for a three-week holiday and I received the call from his boss, the executive director.

I knew the executive director well, as I had been in his top talent group with five others. His team had seen me as an up-and-coming executive and for the last year, I had been attending his face-to-face meetings, taking on projects from his office and being coached by his chief of staff.

Basically, as soon as my boss's plane was in the air, I got the call from him. He told me he had a general manager role, that he wanted me to undertake for up to six months. He had wanted to ask me to do it for a few weeks, but he knew my boss wouldn't let him take me. So as soon as he knew my boss was away and he couldn't have any input into it, he rang me.

I said yes to the job and couldn't stop laughing at the way this organisation and some of the egos worked in this part of the company. It was a privilege to be asked and I was in the city on Monday being shown the ropes of my new secondment.

The new general manager role, my first GM role ever, was to lead the Contract Management Group. The team had around 100 employees, mainly located in Brisbane. They had accountability for the contracts in the field and were responsible for monitoring their performance.

Most of the contracts were related to large construction work, where large equipment like a bulldozer, diggers and pothole diggers were needed. We also had other contracts like uniforms and tool-related contracts. It was another part of the business that I was aware of, had worked on some projects like uniforms, but mostly I wasn't aware of the day-to-day tasks they performed.

The guy who held the role before me was moving into a director's role in New South Wales, so he was only a phone call away and we had developed a good rapport.

To introduce me to the team, he held a face-to-face meeting in Sydney for me. He was from Sydney, along with some of my new direct reports.

The meeting enabled me to understand what their key projects, drivers and performance looked like. I also got to know the new staff and understand who the biggest voices were.

My new direct reports were all big personalities. I had never come across a group that had so many opinions, weren't afraid to speak up and tell each other what they thought and, in some cases, sit and sulk when their idea wasn't taken into consideration. Controlling the conversations and direction took a lot of work, and it was quite a stressful time.

The other thing that got to me was when meetings were over, and someone didn't like the outcome, they would either march into my office and tell me what I should've done or tell me what I now needed to do. It was all quite condescending. I felt like no one had my back. My executive director who I now reported to was putting a lot of pressure on me, but this was a whole new level.

Most of the time, in the first two months, I hated coming to work. I would complain to Robert about the big personalities, that I was losing control, they didn't respect me and I didn't know how to rein them in. But Robert being Robert, he would tell me to do what I had always done. This group was no different, they were a new group of egos and you needed to stand up and be the leader. Be the person they want you to be.

I was still a bit fearful of pushing my way through and across this group. I could tell already that some of their teams worked well but others didn't. They all had different styles and I did come to understand that I had one manager that had my back. Most days we would have catch-ups to discuss what he was hearing on the ground and I would then make the decisions about what I needed to do next.

I really liked him having my back, we started to plan out a face-to-face meeting which we were going to hold in Brisbane at the end of October. I would outline the direction of our team's strategy with him leading it, so that I can gain some respect and control. I felt like this meeting was going to be the fresh start that the team and I needed.

But, as always, my perfect plan to gain the trust and confidence of my team came crashing down. When I arrived in Brisbane, I received a phone call from my manager asking me to get back on a plane to Melbourne as our contractor workforce had decided to strike. The strike had been driven from their association on a platform of fair pay for a fair day's work. They had decided they were going on strike indefinitely from tomorrow.

I told my manager I wasn't going back to Melbourne, that it was a waste of time and I would manage it from Brisbane. I made phone calls to our three suppliers, asked them what they were going to do to manage the strike. They knew that if most of the workforce did strike then hundreds, maybe thousands, of customers would be affected that week.

They gave me their feedback, and although I trusted it, my team told me that it was all bullshit, that they were just telling me what I wanted to hear and this would only get worse.

On day one of the strike, nearly 90 per cent of the workers did strike, or were harassed to the point that they didn't complete a full day's work. For the 10 per cent who didn't, it was because they had mouths to feed at home. The strike was in the news, I was on so many hookups and phone calls trying to understand what the suppliers were doing to get their workers back to work and a boss that was yelling at me down the phone.

I basically had to stop the face-to-face meeting and put a control centre in place. We made phone calls all day trying to get the status of workers for the next few days. Day after day, more workers returned to work, but we had a group that was pretty determined to play this out. Mostly the workers in Melbourne were the ones that stayed out and caused the impact to our customers.

By Friday, I hadn't been able to get much sleep, but I had gotten a better picture of who was able to stand up to work through these situations. I had done a lot of crying and I didn't know if I could come back next week and lead this team. I had made some mistakes during that week in trying to manage my team and my suppliers. I felt that I wasn't strong enough for this role and most of my direct reports, except a couple, seemed to think that as well.

Throughout the week, all I had heard from my boss was to do this, do that. He was more frantic than anyone in the team. He had made a few threats to me, which I ignored. I was worried that if things didn't settle down on Wednesday, as it was the Melbourne Cup public holiday on the Tuesday, then I would probably be moved out of the role.

During this time, I also had several calls with the manager before myself. He did give me a lot of advice of how to manage the individual suppliers. He also told me to separate our boss's reaction, his panic and gave me some insight to how everyone was feeling about how I was handling the situation.

On Friday night, Robert arrived from Melbourne as we were going down to Byron Bay for a weekend with some friends from Brisbane. I was taking Monday off and was going to a race function on Melbourne Cup Day on the Gold Coast. We were flying out of the Gold Coast on Wednesday morning at 6 am and I would be in the office by 10 am.

Over that four-day weekend, I was happy to put my worries behind me and enjoy time with my friends. I know I drank too much alcohol but who cared. I did receive some phone calls from my boss on the Monday, except for Melbourne, most of the workers were back at work in the other states. I frocked up on Melbourne Cup Day and had another great day.

On Wednesday morning, Robert and I got up early and flew back to Melbourne. I reached the office by 10 am with my boss waiting for me. Face-to-face he was a gentle giant, he had more front when he was on the phone to you. We discussed what had happened, how I had handled it. Personally, I didn't think anyone could've handled it better. By now 90 per cent of the workers were back at work and now we had the job of asking them to work extra hours over the next two weeks to attend all the customers that had been delayed.

I kept my job and was told that it had been a steep learning curve and my peers had said that I did a decent job in getting the workforce back via the suppliers. I was happy to hear that, but it still made me feel sick in the stomach wondering if he was just giving me lip service. Was he keeping me in the role because I was a woman or because what he was saying was true?

On the Wednesday, one of my managers who worked for me was in the office. He sat in my office, with his big ego, and told me everything that I should have done. He was quite condescending and certainly very intimidating. He was double my age, had been in the company double the time and, reading between the lines, was basically telling me he could've done better.

During the conversation, I didn't know whether to yell at him and tell him to get out or cry. I decided to let him have his say and just nod. When he left my office, giving me a hug with a smile on his face,

I was angry and devastated. What was he saying behind my back? I knew he was undermining me and he was after my job.

I quickly got up from my desk and decided to get some fresh air. I didn't need this shit. I didn't need to be told what to do; I needed a team to support me. I went to the park, yes, the same one I went to all those years ago when the shit hit the fan. I didn't cry as much, but I did shed a tear. Then I pulled myself together asked two of my managers to get on the phone in the next 15 minutes, as I needed to talk to them urgently.

Once the three of us were on the phone, I was open about the previous conversation I had had with one of their colleagues. They weren't surprised because he had already asked the rest of the team how they thought I performed under pressure. Only one person totally agreed with him; the others said it was a team effort and that they should've shown better support to me.

We debriefed the events from the previous week, going through everything we had done, what we could've done differently and decided to do a written review. I would then present that to my boss and peers about how we could change the way we reacted in the future. What some of my team didn't know is that I knew this structure wasn't working, my operations manager and his colleague knew it too, and we were going to present a different structure for the future.

Before Christmas, I presented the findings to my boss and peer group. We then discussed how we could incorporate these functions into the field groups and disband most of my team. The team wasn't working. They didn't take the operational functions to drive performance to the level they needed to. The field needed to take on this accountability like they did with their own teams.

It was agreed that we would work on a new structure that would be implemented in the field. I would announce a restructure in early 2009 and drive the implementation with the field directors. This meant that the managers that weren't supporting the group to the level needed would need to find new jobs and those who were and were driving suppliers successfully would form a smaller team that managed the contract, not the operational performance.

In early February 2009, I flew to Brisbane with my managers, who by now had been briefed on what we were instructing the staff on the following day. On the Tuesday, I stood in front of the staff and briefed our employees on the changes. Some would find roles within the new structure, while most would be placed within the wider company, but this was a better way to drive performance.

A couple of my managers didn't like the way I addressed the staff. One even came up to me and said, 'You didn't even say thanks to them for the years of service and the work they have done to date.' Whether this was right or wrong I turned to him and said that 'I didn't think the work they had been doing was up to standard, and that we have already had this discussion, so that's why I didn't say it'. He wasn't happy and I know he went and told his staff what I said which I found very unprofessional.

I ended up making that manager and the previous opinionated manager redundant. One found a new role in the company, the other one left angry and I was very happy to see the back of him. He wasn't right for the job; he didn't know how to manage staff and his performance was appalling. He probably would have been sacked; he was lucky to leave with a few extra dollars.

The work I had done with this group and the restructure impressed my boss and his colleague. My peers were happy and at our next face-to-face with them, they congratulated me. Everyone was happy and I had learnt so many lessons taking on this group. I had secured some trust and respect from my peers and I was ready to take on the newly formed team. But that wasn't to be.

On the 13th of March, the last day of my face-to-face with my peers, my boss' colleague, another executive director, asked me to catch up with him before the end of the meeting. We went into an office, and he told me he had been impressed with how he had seen me perform over the last few years. That what I had done in the contracts team was a great piece of work and offered me a general managers role with him.

I nearly passed out. I didn't really know this man – by all accounts, most of the time I feared him, as did a lot of my peers in my current team, or they had negative things to say about him and his team.

The role was an enablement group role. It had four separate functions, predominately back of house functions for the field. I would have six direct reports and around 350 staff across the nation undertaking various roles. The job could be done in Melbourne, but most of the staff were in Brisbane. I would have to travel to Brisbane regularly as he believed the culture up there needed some change and that from what he had seen with my Melbourne work ethic, I could do it.

He also said that if I wanted to, I could move to Brisbane, all expenses paid. Included in the package would be six months' rent and the ability to take my husband's car up as well.

Wow, I hadn't been expecting that. He told me I could think about it over the weekend, talk to my husband. I already knew I wanted to take it. I didn't know if Robert wanted to go to Brisbane, or if he could get a job up there. Robert had been offered to go to Brisbane back in 2003, but he knocked it back because I didn't want to leave our family and friends. But I had a different line of thought now, and this could be a great opportunity.

I told him I would take it on the spot. I would talk to Robert about it that night, which was also Robert's birthday, so this was going to be a big surprise. My new boss then told my existing boss and said he wanted to announce to the team while everyone was in the room. Although my existing boss was sad, he also understood why I wanted the role and that I deserved it.

We re-entered the room and announced that I was going to be taking up a new role under the newly formed structure within the business. This would enable me to consider moving to Brisbane and I would be an asset to the new team with all my field experience.

I was over the moon; everyone was so happy for me, and I couldn't stop smiling. This was my first general manager role. The money was going to be fantastic and again I had moved up the next step in the ladder by showing my highly driven work ethic and how I improved performance and made the necessary changes in the business that would drive a better outcome for our customers.

That night, I met Robert at a pub and told him the good news. He was happy but shocked, and we had more drinks to celebrate both his birthday and my promotion. Over the weekend, I made lots of calls to my parents and friends announcing my new promotion. They were all overjoyed.

The first couple of months in my new job were extremely exhausting. I had a new team to manage, a new group of peers and a new boss. I was also travelling to Brisbane every second or third week for the week. Getting a 6 am flight from Melbourne on Monday morning, a 4 pm flight from Brisbane on Friday afternoons.

During that week, I worked night and day. I stayed in a hotel that had a kitchenette and mostly ate Lean Cuisine. My hotel was a 15-minute walk to the office. I deliberately booked that one so I would get some sort of exercise and a couple of nights a week, I would do some extra walking before dinner around the Brisbane River.

I also had a couple of face-to-face meetings with my new team and drove out to Toowoomba and the Gold Coast to meet other team members. The work was great, I loved learning the new functions by sitting with our people. I had a new assistant who I needed to get to know and I loved the warmer weather in Brisbane.

After the fourth trip to Brisbane, and after meeting Robert in the city where he had been drinking with our friends at a pub, I was already over the long weeks of being away. I always came home to Robert out on Friday night, meaning I would have to drive us home and our weekends together just didn't seem to be long enough.

After the fifth trip, I told Robert I wanted us to go to Brisbane. To my shock, he agreed immediately. He could see that I was tired and grumpy after being away. That I was doing so much work from home at night after the trips and this could be a great opportunity to move to a new city and kick off the next part of our lives.

Over the past year, we had been trying to get pregnant, which wasn't happening. I began to think the heavy workloads and stress was playing a part and you can't really get pregnant if your prime time of the month is when you are sitting in a hotel room 1,800 kilometres away from each other.

We made the decision that we would move in August of that year, and we told our family and friends about our plans. Our dogs would go to my parents until we got settled and all our possessions would move with me. Robert's boss had told him he couldn't transfer his job up to Brisbane and he would have to find a new one himself. Robert then moved in with his brother until he found a job in Brisbane and we would see each other every three weeks.

Robert's brother had just moved back from Japan and they had had their first baby in April 2009. His brother did a lot of trips back to Japan, so having Robert staying with his sister-in-law and niece worked quite well for all of them.

On the first Saturday in August, we had a going-away party and drank as much of the alcohol we had as we couldn't take open bottles in the truck. For the next two weeks, we cleaned out the house, had a garage sale and the removalists came and took our belongings to Brisbane on the 20th of August. We then moved into Robert's brother's place for a couple of days, before taking the flight to Brisbane on the 25th of August to start our new adventure.

We had found a unit only five kilometres out of the city near a railway line. It was also only an hour to the Gold Coast where our good friends lived so I could visit them on weekends. The unit was great and had shops around the corner and I was finally going to get the necessary rest I needed.

Even though Robert was going to be living in Melbourne, we planned out our weekends based on my work travel and Robert's job so that we could see each other every three weeks. This meant we were only going to be away from each other for two weeks at a time.

It was also great for me, as I had so much work to be done with the new team. I was able to spend longer hours at work, have a team meeting with them, design the new strategy for the team and work from home at night.

It was an exciting time, and I really loved my new team. Because they were spread out around the country, I rolled out our new strategy via video, to every location. The teams had never seen this before and they enjoyed the sessions and Q&A. I then decided to make videos so that they could hear from me regularly. I travelled interstate to see the teams, mainly focusing on the ones where we had weaker team managers so I could chat to them about what they needed to improve.

In October, two months after we moved, and on a weekend when Robert was in Brisbane, we bought a house. It was 10 kilometres east of the city, a post-war Queenslander that Robert had so many ideas of extending, renovating and putting a pool in. We were over the moon, but even happier when Robert got a job and moved to Brisbane in November.

We were moving into our new house the week before Christmas, so it was perfect to have Robert up here to be part of that. It was also our 10-year wedding anniversary at the end of November, so we went to Thailand for 10 days to celebrate. I couldn't wait for our life together to begin in Brisbane. We couldn't have been happier.

Throughout 2010, life was amazing. We were making new friends, visiting our friends on the Gold Coast regularly and receiving quite a few visits from our families and friends too. We were still making regular trips to Melbourne and I was working hard in my role and travelling for work, but not as much as I had been the previous year.

In the middle of 2010, I was asked to undertake the field director role for Queensland while he took leave. Part of me moving to Brisbane, was to be on the succession plan for this role and do relief when it was available. I had been told their succession in Queensland wasn't strong and I would be a great person to start to undertake relief, with the possibility of taking on that role sometime in the future.

I was in the role for three weeks, and during that time, I mostly got to know the managers, went on one field trip down to the Northern NSW and went to a few team meetings in Brisbane to understand the performance and how my teams could assist them further.

The managers in this team were great, they were engaging, respectful and responsive. The three weeks flew by and although I didn't think I did much and had no impact, getting to know the people was a great opportunity for me.

Over the past 18 months, I had learnt so much from my new manager. He was a very intelligent man, had lots of great ideas and insight and he very rarely got upset. He was very respectful and I was surprised how much I enjoyed working for him.

In late 2010, another restructure was looming. We had decided to decentralise some functions and I had to lose a manager, one that didn't want to go. He was very disgruntled and didn't take the news of being redundant well. When I told him face-to-face in my office he started yelling. The staff on the floor could hear him outside and were worried about me.

He told me that it wasn't fair, that I was doing this on purpose and he knew I never liked him. That this was a personal decision, and I would regret it. I let him rant and get his anger out. The whole time he was yelling, I was scared. I had my hands clasped in my lap, pushing them together trying not to show any fear. My face was straight, again trying not to let any fear rise or show. He then asked me if that was it, if that was all I had to say, which I confirmed and he stood up, opened the door and walked out.

The staff outside were so happy to see me and that I was unharmed. I was so happy that he hadn't bounded over the desk as I thought it might happen at one point. It was quite a traumatic discussion and really shook me up, but I tried not to let it get to me and gave him some time to work through it. On the day he left, he didn't say much but he was respectful. Making people redundant is hard on both parties.

Not long after this restructure, I was asked to assist the director in Queensland after the 2011 floods. The floods had devastated most of

Brisbane and several towns out west and to the north. The arrangement was that he would manage the flood areas and I would manage Northern NSW, Central and Northern Queensland. They hadn't been affected, but the current manager couldn't lead the whole region.

It was a great opportunity to work side-by-side with the current director and get to know more about the region. A lot of work needed to happen during this time, plus media commitments by him, so it made sense for me to come in and help.

MIDDLE MANAGEMENT

I was about to go back to my role six weeks later when Cyclone Yasi hit. It devastated the northern coast of Queensland, wiping out towns and islands. Again, I was asked to assist while the current director took on that. I was then asked to continue the work that was happening in the flooded areas of Brisbane where permanent works were continuing and ensure the region south of Rockhampton continued to deliver its workload.

Then, in May of 2011, after the current director was asked to take on a new role as the lead of customer service for the company, I was asked to take on the regional role. I was so excited. It was for six months initially, and I could lead the team the way that I wanted. This was a dream come true, and at 38 years of age, it wasn't what I had expected to be doing.

I took it on the way I wanted to do it. I didn't change much initially. I understood how the team operated, visited lots of teams and did a lot of one-on-ones with the managers.

It became apparent that the teams in the field wanted to see me more, so I wrote a plan that saw me visit the 50-odd teams that were in my structure once a year. I could see four teams a week and schedule one week a month to be out on the road. My team in Brisbane kept the business running while I was out in the field. I really enjoyed being able to spend time with my managers, team managers and staff and building a rapport face-to-face.

When I went down to New South Wales, I could drive about 1,500 kilometres in a week. Thankfully, I had a Toyota Prado 4WD do it in. My trips to Northern Queensland would be out west to Charleville, north to Mt Isa and on the coast to Cooktown. Every place was different, and every staff member was different, but, overall, with my monthly videos and updates, I received some great feedback. It wasn't long before we started to see improvement in engagement and performance in the field.

My managers were great most of the time. They didn't get away with much, especially when performance wasn't hitting the mark. When we were asked to reduce the workforce in 2011, my managers and I decided that, instead of making lots of people redundant in the 2012 financial year, the team would dig deep, and we ended up sacking over 50 people for all types of actions that weren't in line with the company's rules. Some of these were for criminal actions and although it was hard, it was the right thing to do.

I supported my managers with the help of my human resources manager, where it became apparent that some individuals were not doing the right thing. We exited 10 per cent of the field workforce, we increased engagement by addressing behaviours that others knew about and productivity lifted again.

In April 2012, whilst hosting a face-to-face in Brisbane with my team, my boss's boss, the Chief Operating Officer (COO), was in Brisbane. He had asked me to join him with other executives in Brisbane for an informal chat. I went to meet him in a meeting room with around 15 other colleagues and he was talking about a great employee who he was honoured to promote. By the time he got the words out, everyone was looking at me and he said, 'Congratulations! I am here today on behalf of the company to announce that Suzanne Gomes is being promoted to the role of director of field services.'

I was so overwhelmed that I burst into tears. Everyone was clapping for me in the room and telling me how deserved this appointment was. After the catch up he then took me to a meeting room and put a stack of papers in front of me. I couldn't believe that after 12 months of performing this role that I absolutely loved, I was going to be offered it permanently. I again thanked him so much and as I was shaking, I signed my name on the papers which was my new remuneration. He then told me we needed to tell my team and would announce it to them.

I then took him back to my team and he made the announcement. I burst into tears again, thanking them for all their hard work, their support and commitment to me and hoped they were happy that I was now their permanent manager. Everyone was so happy for me and thanked the COO for appointing me. We had driven some great initiatives and now I could do even more.

The next 12 months were much the same: visiting staff, improving performance and managing business politics. My three interstate colleagues were sometimes hard to work with. I protected my team a lot and kept them away from most of it. We had a job to do, and I had an awesome general manager who supported our strategy. There was always lots to do, but as a team, I loved coming to work, doing the hard yards and reaping the rewards with my team.

It didn't take long for me to gain a lot of recognition from my boss, the COO and a number of executives in the business. I was asked to do a few speaking events, be part of some great projects and continually work with my peers to improve the business. I had the best life in Queensland with Robert, moving into some great roles. I couldn't be more grateful.

My Lesson for You:

- The only constant, in business is change. Be prepared to change your business every one to three years.
- If someone believes you can do it, give it a go.
- Spend time on the business, not in the business. When you are the leader, you are not the technical expert – your experts work for you.
- Make sure your team understands the strategy, the vision, team values and the non-negotiables. Continually refer back to this. Everything you do has to link back to the strategy.
- Manage your emotions. If you are having trouble managing your reactions, then engage an expert. I engaged a counsellor to help me to believe in myself and help me through the tough times.
- Make time for healthy eating, exercise, mindfulness and time outside of work. You are the master of your time.

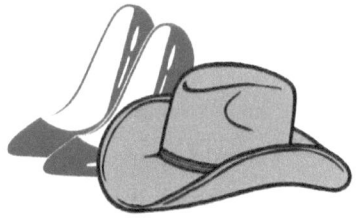

Chapter 5

One Chick, Many Men

I've had conflicting feelings about writing this chapter. I haven't known how much to tell and in how much detail, but I've decided to write it nevertheless – and please know that this is only a reflection on 1 to 2 per cent of the men that I worked with.

In a lot of ways, I loved working with men. They very rarely got caught up in their emotions, which at times was great but could also be frustrating.

Most of the time they welcomed me into their teams and worked well with me. They were respectful and polite towards me as their leader.

What I am about to tell you does not define me, but it helped me to be the person I am today. To be able to stand up for myself. Not because of the men, but rather because of who I wanted to be.

Unfortunately, there is still a lot of sexism in company culture. I don't know how we will ever stop that. As you read this chapter, you might not like the way I dealt with some of these situations, but neither did I at times.

As you read these stories, I would appreciate if you don't criticise me, but take them as learnings – to teach your sons, your people, the men that you live or work with every day on how to respect their colleagues in the workplace. These are stories that need to be told to educate the next generation of leaders.

I started out working in a call centre which was female centric. About a third of the call centre employees were men and were spread across several different roles within the centre. When the opportunity to go over to the depot and take on a secondment for six months was offered to me, I took it immediately.

Although I wasn't the first choice – I was fourth in line after three females knocked the role back – I didn't bat an eye lid before saying yes. A call centre isn't the greatest place to work. Every second call you receive you are typically abused and you never know what you're going to have to deal with during the next one.

My father, my uncle and cousins had worked in that side of the business. My dad said it would be a great place to work. Not only did I get along with my colleagues in the depot, but I also met my future husband as you've already heard.

It didn't take long before I was starting to get many opportunities outside of the depot in other positions, and in 2005, I took on my first management role leading 180 staff with 12 team leaders. I think for many of these men, it was the first time they had been led by a female, so a few of them were as nervous as I was.

Several of the team managers were already aware of me, and some had even worked with me when I worked for one of my colleagues. For the team managers and some staff, I had naturally taken the next step after undertaking a few manager secondments. Others saw me as the new girl on the block and I am sure there were many comments questioning my ability to lead such a team.

I was naturally nervous when I first moved into the role. I took the time to meet with each manager individually. I held face-to-face meetings to get to know the guys and it didn't take long before my couch in my office become a counselling chair.

I would have my managers come in and talk to me about anything and everything – from people in our team to performance issues, to their children and sometimes their marriages.

One team manager said to me that he felt so comfortable being able to talk to someone who would listen, acknowledge him and work with him to provide real solutions, rather than just saying, 'Everything will be OK, mate.' That was typically how men responded.

I think I was a breath of fresh air for the men who told me they had never been given support like this before.

But not everyone who worked for my team was as welcoming. We are talking about men that have only worked with men. I never knew their backgrounds, upbringing or what their fathers, uncles or mothers had taught them about dealing with and respecting women. I made sure to tread lightly when I first started to attend their team meetings and listened to what they had to say.

I also had to remember that maybe some of these guys hadn't been listened to in the past. Maybe they were frustrated because some of the issues that had been in the field for years hadn't been addressed and what was I going to do about it. Not because I was a woman, but because I was another manager who was coming in to promise the world yet give them nothing.

I was never offended when there might be heightened voices or someone who displayed passion. But when the tone changed from passion to disrespect, which for me was easy to identify, the game changed.

My first experience of disrespect was at a team meeting in 2005. I had gone out to one of the outer city teams. Again, I was a bit reserved, and whenever I met a new team, I would introduce myself by telling them who I was, what I had done and what my objectives were for our teams and customers.

One guy didn't want to hear about it – 'Promises, promises and nothing more,' he said. When I told him I needed them to give me a chance, that we would be implementing this strategy and I would be back on a regular basis to understand how it is going, he wasn't satisfied. He just told me that he was 'sick of fucking management telling us how to do our jobs.'

Now, I hadn't been sworn at work before, so suddenly, my face went red and I boiled over. I had listened to this guy for long enough, he wasn't respecting me or his team, so I responded with, 'Well, why don't you fucking see what I do before jumping to fucking conclusions?' He then turned around to me, and I can still remember his voice saying, 'Don't you swear at me.' I turned around and said, 'Well, don't fucking swear at me first.'

Looking down the table straight into this man's eyes, my hands were shaking. I couldn't believe what I had just said, much less what was to come. All I got was a shake of the head, a few smiles from some of the other guys and finally some silence and we continued the meeting.

After the meeting, I spoke to the team manager about this guy's behaviour. I got told it was typical of him, and from what I could see, the team managers had let it go on for years. This was the first time he had had to deal with a backhander and especially one from a woman. From then, I knew I could match it with the 1-2 per cent of the guys that didn't want to work with me. But most thought, 'She doesn't put up with crap, good on her!'

When I moved to Queensland and took over the leadership role for Queensland and Northern NSW, I came across another culture of men. Country guys, who may have to drive 500 kilometres to see one customer. They travel the outback, islands beyond our shores and places that most Australians will never see.

They work with customers who have grown up on the land, seen hardships of drought and floods and who, at times, don't like seeing people. It was such an eye-opener to see the true heroes of our land, of the company that I worked for, that made sure the customer came first.

When I took over the leadership role, not only was I a woman, but I was also a previous call centre consultant. I had come from Victoria, and Victoria doesn't have what we have, plus I had never worked in the field before. My portfolio from Victoria didn't mean much and I had to earn their respect. In some ways, I didn't mind that. Some of these guys didn't like management – I got it, I just wanted them to know that I couldn't fix everything. I certainly couldn't fix the past, but I would do my finest with my team to do whatever I can now. At the end of the day, what I did promise is that I would always give them an answer.

In 2013, I went up north to undertake a road trip with my team. These usually meant going out with the manager and team managers. Meet as many staff as possible across 500 kilometres in a week. Going out and working in the rain, heat, whatever it took to help them do their jobs, get to know what was happening in the teams and hopefully gain the respect that I needed to lead the them. Plus, I loved visiting some amazing places that I had never been before.

This one trip was wet – tropical wet. We started in Cairns and drove down to Townsville, meeting staff along the way and when we got there it was pouring with rain. I am sure the guy I went out with on day three of my trip would've rather sat in the depot all afternoon, but we had customers to service, and they didn't care if we got wet – plus, we had raincoats and umbrellas to keep us dry.

On day four, we drove south in extreme rain and wind, cyclonic conditions, to visit staff in Proserpine. We stopped a few times on the side of the road as we couldn't see two feet in front of us. We went through water that was so strong I thought it was going to take us off the road. It was one of the only times while driving when I have been scared for my life. All this just to see the next team, to sit down with them and resolve some of their issues.

We turned up at the depot to have breakfast with the guys before the meeting. My heart was still pounding, and recalling the previous day's trip, I felt so grateful that we had made it to Proserpine. One guy had made up his mind that he was going to give all the managers in the room a piece of his mind and he didn't care how he did it.

His swearing and disrespect for us, the company and some of his team were just despicable. He couldn't have been more of a pig. His abuse was something I had never come across before – yes, even worse than the guy in Melbourne. Now, this wasn't passion, he was just being rude. We were trying to work with him, but he was swearing like a trooper and once he dropped the 'c-word', that was it.

I remember telling him to either get out or shut up. He then told me I didn't care! Well, that was it – he got a barrage from me. I am not proud of what came next, but I have never been so angry with a staff member before. Was my response inappropriate? Yes. But I wasn't going to put up with that type of behaviour.

I told him that I had risked my life in a car to be here. I said, 'I could've got on a plane and gone home. I could've missed this meeting and gone back to my husband. But no, I decided to come here, speak to all of you in a civilised, open-minded manner and this is what I cop for doing that.' The team managers and manager tried to pacify the situation, but again I told them to keep out of it, 'This was between him and I because now it was personal. Don't you dare tell me I don't care!'

So, not my finest moment, but I deserved some respect and this pig of a man wasn't giving it. The guy stayed in the meeting and decided to shut up. Now, it did make the room a little tense, but we got back on track and I decided to give my attention to the rest of the team – hopefully he would stay quiet.

At the end of the meeting when I went to go and speak to him one on one, he basically ran out of the meeting room. I had two of his colleagues step in front of me saying, 'Leave it Suzanne, let him calm down.' I didn't want to leave it, but by the time they stalled me, I reached the car park and he was gone.

Most of the time, when outbursts happened within teams, other team members would come up to me and apologise for the guy's behaviour and say, 'Please don't think that reflects the team.' I had one team that basically gave a guy a mouthful out in the car park because of what he said to me. I even had a few guys apologise to me after the meeting, in which I told them the behaviour wasn't necessary and they just needed to give me a chance; that was all I asked for.

After the incident in Proserpine, that was a moment where I decided that I didn't want to be that sort of manager, that I didn't want to have a reputation for attacking staff. These incidents had happened at different levels during different meetings throughout my career. I was getting sick of being abused, but I realised that giving the same behaviour back wasn't what I should be doing. I needed to change tack and start to respond to them with a level of control.

I must emphasise this again: this reflected only one to two per cent of the staff. It was not a reflection of the culture and certainly not of the company's values. The company was very strong on talking about their values and ensuring their staff worked by them. But every so often there would be a couple of guys that didn't have strong values. I always wondered what they were like at home.

It wasn't just swearing and abuse a couple of times a year that I witnessed. I also witnessed a side of a few men that did try to take it too far. The odd wolf whistle, a tap on the arse, a guy who tapped me on the arse in front of my husband and a couple of guys even tried to kiss me.

Now, these are people who I would deal with on a regular basis. They knew I was married; some of them even knew my husband as he worked for the same company. But that didn't stop them from wanting to put their hands on me. Again, this is not a reflection of the company. When alcohol is involved, which it was at social events, the true colours of some individuals emerged.

On all these occasions, I yelled at them, tried to slap them, pushed them away and never engaged in their behaviour. I threatened that if they did it again, I would take it to my boss or human resources. But I never actually filed a complaint. I didn't do it, because I was more scared of what Robert would think of me and what he might do to them. If I could control their behaviour and they never did it to me again, then I would deal with it.

At the time, I never thought about what it might mean for other women. Would they do it to other women, and if they did, how would those women respond? I couldn't believe in some cases that they had the audacity to do these things. I don't think I ever gave the wrong impression to these guys, and I know that isn't the right thing to say, as no one should ever feel they provoked that kind of behaviour, but at the time I was just one of the guys. I never saw the two sexes as being distinct from one another in the workplace and I never expected these men to touch me inappropriately.

As I said at the start of this chapter, it is not my intention to suggest that this was the overall culture. It certainly wasn't. I have had several managers work for me, and with me, that are my good mates. They have protected me and given me a lot of care and support especially when my husband was sick. I couldn't have asked for better friends, but there were just a few that couldn't keep their hands and thoughts to themselves.

I never asked these guys after the fact why they thought they could do that. Why did they think they could take advantage of me? In some ways, it was like going to a pub or nightclub and someone hitting you on the arse, but these people knew me. Well, I thought they knew what I stood for, what I valued and that it wasn't acceptable to act like that towards me.

In a big company, there are many affairs, inuendoes and rumours that you hear about. I had heard a few rumours about myself from colleagues who I was friends with. Going to the shop for lunch or a beer after work with a few work mates, work mates that are guys, can really get the tongues wagging. But to think they could take it one step further always blew me away.

I do think a couple of the guys were quite remorseful for what they did or tried to do. They were always so respectful and supportive after these times. I don't think it was just because they were worried about me reporting them. I hope it was because they reflected on it and were embarrassed.

I will never know, as I never asked, but from the next day, week or month that I saw them again, they certainly hadn't forgotten about their behaviour because they would avoid me in some part. That is what I believe because it never happened from the same person again. I sent them a very strong message. I will not put up with that, don't you ever do that again.

One of them apologised straight after he tried to touch me, and we talked about what was going on in their life that caused him to act out so irresponsibly. I know if they ever read this book, they will be so remorseful for what they tried to do and I would never tell anyone who they were – not now nor the future.

I know he learnt a very valuable lesson out of this situation and he totally respects the reaction I gave him, plus the talk afterwards. I am also not saying because he had a lot of issues going on in his life that what he did was acceptable. But at least he had enough respect to talk to me about it straight after. It made a world of difference and I still talk to him when I see him today.

ONE CHICK, MANY MEN

As I said, the main reason I didn't say anything was because Robert worked for the same company and he knew some of these people. He had worked with some of them and of course I talked about them at home. If he had have known what went on, I think he would've approached them and said something.

When the incident happened in front of Robert, I thought he was going to knock the guy out. We left the event shortly after. I didn't need Robert to worry about me. I could hold my own and if it had of happened a second time with any of them, I certainly would've reported it. Would I have told Robert? Probably not, because he was so protective of me, and I didn't need him to lose his job.

Now, after reading all this, you may have different thoughts on my approach and response to these guys. I know some people may say, 'Well, its people like you who don't formally address it that allow it to continue.' Yes, that may be the case, but I don't want this to be a chapter that reflects my overall corporate life, as it certainly wasn't.

I learnt a lot from these events. I knew I could stand up for myself. It taught me that if you disrespect or step on my values then I won't put up with it. It probably did make me a stronger, as well as more cautious. I did accept the times when my mates said they would walk me back to my room, to my car. That's the thing, 99 per cent of the guys I worked with respected me, supported me and some are still great mates to this day. I would do the same for them if they asked.

Over time, I think I won more hearts and minds than I did enemies. The guys that worked for me liked my approach, valued my opinions and honesty and they stood up for me on several occasions. They respected me for fighting the good fight when it was needed and that I was not scared to stand up for what I thought was right. They didn't do this because I was a woman; they did it because they respected me as their leader!

My Lesson for You:

- Don't ever let someone bully you, speak down to you or disrespect you.
- Politely ask them to refrain from using that tone when speaking to you.
- Never talk back in the same language they are using. It doesn't work and you won't feel good about it.
- If someone in your team is angry, ensure you find out why. What is going on for them and why are they so upset? It's important to understand this, as that person may be crying out for help.
- If you are touched inappropriately report it. Don't let them get away with it. It is disrespectful and no one deserves to be attacked.
- Engage a mentor to talk through the tough times.

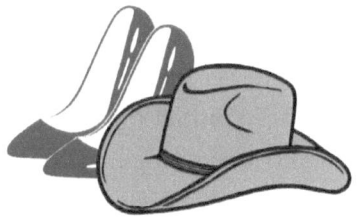

Chapter 6

The Boys' Club

While some organisations may not like to admit it, you do come across boys' clubs in corporate culture. Especially in the operations or engineering parts of those businesses. I don't think it is because they make it like that, but when there are large groups of men working together, playing sport together, being mates – well, they act in a boys' club way. Does it mean that they are rude to woman in that environment? No, most of the time they aren't, but when you are the only woman in a room of 10 men, you certainly notice it.

After taking on my first leadership role, I started to see the differences in the ways in which I acted, presented and lead my team, compared to how men did. Now, what I am about to say isn't against men for acting this way – most don't even realise they are doing it.

From what I understand, men have typically been groomed by their parents to be the breadwinner (especially in the baby boomer era). They are very self-assured, goal-centric, and very competitive, they need recognition and rewards and they are workaholics to their own detriment.

So, along comes a woman who isn't competitive, wants to collaborate, listens, passes on rewards to her teams and just gets shit done. I am sure you can already see the conflict that would start to ruminate in my head. It starts to sound something like, 'God, some of these men are egotistic, pigheaded, authoritarian and put themselves in front of their teams.'

I wasn't one who wanted to compete with the boys. I wanted to develop my teams with true teamwork, working together to achieve the team goal. Not the individual goals, because last one over the line wins in my world, not the first. I wanted my people to help each other to achieve and to work with our people to achieve it.

I always felt that my approach was different to my colleagues. But on the flip side I wanted to be seen as hard but fair. I was happy to coach my teams to succeed. I was happy to mentor my people to deliver, to coach my people to develop their skills. But if you didn't identify issues, didn't work on yourself and with your team and if I identified you weren't fit for the role then there would be a different conversation around what role would be right for them.

I also didn't like egos in my team. Several times, I had a team member who glossed over issues. They were focusing on the high points but not the areas of concern. In our business, all performance results counted. If we were in a meeting and someone was trying to avoid the gap, issue, blocker, then I wasn't backwards in coming forwards to call that out.

I didn't call it out behind doors, which is what some of my male colleagues did. Everyone in my team knew that if you had an issue call it out. Call it, because if you don't then I would in our team performance meetings. It wasn't to embarrass anyone, but these guys were being paid good money and they needed to resolve issues if they wanted to stay in my team.

I also had a very good understanding of everyone's performance in my operations team and where the gaps were. So, if the manager wasn't calling it out, my team would highlight it. If they couldn't start to put actions in place to improve it over a set time, then I would work with my human resources manager to put them on performance improvement plans to enhance their individual outcomes to enable them to become more successful.

Not all managers worked with me on these, then unfortunately, they couldn't be part of the team if they couldn't deliver. Some people are just not cut out to lead big teams with key performance indicators. Several managers in the past may have been chosen due to tenor, that they were automatically next in line or they lived in the right area to become the next manager. I have found that you can coach a manager, but some people are just not fit for the job.

Mostly, the boys' club was in the team I was in, they were my peers. What I worked out is that I had to be stronger. I had to stand up and voice my opinion. I knew some days my opinion wasn't considered, but I knew my idea was what was needed. So, I would go off and do it, deliver the results and then restate how I achieved it.

But some people weren't willing to take on other's ideas. They wouldn't even take on their male colleague's ideas. At times, this wasn't a female/male thing, this was an egotistic approach.

I remember being in a meeting with one of my managers and a male colleague and I suggested to him how to approach something in a different way. He blatantly turned around to both of us and said he would never change. He wasn't prepared to put the change in place, and so we had to put up with the status quo. The consultants that were leading our meeting, immediately asked us to take a break, rethink what was happening in our team and look for a solution to move forward.

When we came back together after 15 minutes of, 'I can't believe our boss won't change their approach for what we are being told is what the staff need,' there was no change. He was adamant that how he led us and our teams was how we needed to operate and that was that. For the rest of the time that I worked for him, I was polite and respectful, but my opinion of him had changed.

When times get tough, and there were a lot of tough times, I had to take deep breaths after or even during many meetings. On a regular basis, several of my colleagues would raise their voice or attack others. After these times, I would go and sit in a toilet cubicle. I would talk to myself about finding strength, not letting them see how upset you are and, especially, don't cry.

But on multiple occasions, my passion was overwhelming, and my emotion would boil over, causing tears to fall. It was embarrassing sitting in a room with some of these men, trying to get your point across and to accept what they had to say but have them not acknowledge you, it wasn't always right. At times, their criticism and reaction to me made me want to cry.

Crying always felt like my biggest weakness, and the more I worked with egotistic men, the more they would get under my skin and the emotion would stream down my cheeks.

In 2013, Queensland was hit with floods only two years after the Brisbane 100-year storm and Cyclone Yasi. It felt like we hadn't even got over the 2011 disaster and we were back in it again. But when you are dealing with infrastructure and large customers, weather events are part of what you do.

I went down to Melbourne to a face-to-face team meeting with my colleagues. There were four of us from around the country who led these teams. The purpose of the meeting was to form better relationships, understand each other's issues and be more open and transparent. I remember walking into the meeting in my corporate attire and everyone else was in casual attire. I had been too busy managing a disaster that I hadn't read the memo on casual attire and automatically felt like I was standing out for the wrong reasons.

All the way through day one, I received calls, texts, emails from my team and from our customer service teams. I even had the pressure of some Queensland politicians telling me I should've been on the ground and not in Melbourne. But I tried to manage both and was doing a bad job.

The waterworks really started when we were asked to rate out of 10 how we were feeling. As we went around the room, my three colleagues were saying eight, seven, and when they came to me, I said, 'Two.' Then one of my colleagues said, 'Oh, Suzanne, it can't be that bad?' That was it; I lost control and started to cry. I started to ask them, 'Can you not see that I am not present in this meeting? That I have so much pressure on me right now?' I asked them why they were not helping me, that they were cruising around thinking the world is wonderful. The pressure had got the best of me, and I walked out. I walked out of the building and just walked and walked and walked.

It seemed that I was getting a bit of a reputation for doing this. But there was only so much I could take on days like this. I didn't have my team around me. I didn't have Robert, and I felt alone and completely out of my depth. I was asked a question that I answered honestly, and instead of being told have a can of concrete and toughen up, I wanted their empathy. But they were men, and, well, empathy wasn't given out in abundance in our team.

In several of my peer teams, made up entirely of men, you never got emotional support. Yes, they might ask what they could do and of course it was always action orientated. But when I was overloaded and being pulled from pillar to post, the last thing I wanted to do was admit it was too much. Having someone say, you're doing a good job, let's go for a coffee to take a break, that's what I needed – but I rarely got it from these men.

I learnt later in my career to depend more on my immediate team. To allocate more of the burden across many to lighten the load. To not always feel that I had to be the one to answer everyone's demands – and, before it all gets too much, to take a breath, take a break and recoup your energy.

This was what it was like some days, and typically these situations with my peers would happen multiple times a year. The energy it took to manage them was exhausting, especially when you and your colleagues are on different planets sometimes.

I also used to keep a lot of this behaviour out of my team's sight. They didn't need to know that all wasn't well with my colleagues and me. But they would work it out and because they did like the way I led them, they were always up for doing their extra bit and making our team look great!

Over time, I managed my emotions a bit better with every episode. I was building resilience whilst staying true to my values. If my values were being challenged, it upset me. I was sick and tired of apologising for my emotions. That was who I was, and I should be able to show it.

During this time, I should have engaged a mentor. I don't know why I never did. It would have helped. But every time I thought a female executive may have been the right person, once I introduced myself and started to talk to them, they seemed to let me down. There never seemed to be the right person, they seemed more interested in themselves or their own team, rather than take the time out to mentor me.

I worked with several consultancy teams over my corporate time and most of them gave me their insights of the behaviours they saw from my colleagues. I talked to several consultants one-on-one about how I was managing them and they gave me several tips on how to work with them. It helped, but in hindsight I should have taken them up on regular mentoring sessions or had them put me in touch with a mentor outside of the company to help me work on my resilience and peer leadership.

One feature of being part of these teams was that I worked with several engineers. Now, I have nothing against engineers, but their thinking was very different to mine. We had done a lot of work on being open about how each other's brains worked, but again I was always on the red spectrum (emotion, care, leadership), where they would dominant the blue section (data, engineering, solutions, sometimes authoritarian). During these sessions, we would laugh about it, but in the real work environment their actions and behaviour made me feel inadequate.

I don't think some of these guys ever realised what they were doing and how I felt that they would discredit me by speaking in a technical and systematic language. It made my brain hurt, and if they just talked in simple English instead of trying to big note their engineering degrees, it would've felt more inclusive. I felt that I was chasing my tail during these conversations. I would have to ask more questions of others, even research what they were talking about, so I could keep up with them. I started to feel that I had imposter syndrome among my peers and it was making me overthink why I was there at all.

The one thing I would continually forget was that I wasn't employed in these teams as the engineering expert. I was given these career opportunities because I could lead teams, I drove results, I had empathy and resolved issues and gaps. My attitude was that my team were the ones with the technical expertise, and I would ask them to deliver that part for me. Plus, at an executive level in generalist roles, we weren't employed to be technical experts.

The boys' club also brought with it a level of loneliness. When I was part of a couple of these teams, I felt that I didn't fit in. I would try and fake being one of them, that maybe if I acted more like them in social circles, they might accept me more or work with me on my ideas. But doing that made me feel uncomfortable, and all I could think was that I was an imposter.

On many occasions, I felt that I was having social conversations with people I really didn't click with. But they were my colleagues, and I needed to work with them to deliver outcomes, so I had to network with them otherwise they would never engage with me. I was the one always walking up to them. It made me feel inferior and I would question myself continually on whether I was worthy to be standing next to them in the same team. Some days, I felt like a fraud.

Then the worst thing happened to me: My thoughts of being a fraud were explicitly spelled out to me by my manager.

When my husband was diagnosed with leukaemia in 2013 and needed a bone marrow transplant a year later, I took three months off work. He needed a full-time carer and I wanted to be that for him.

After I returned to work, I realised quite quickly that I wasn't going back to my original job. Not because I couldn't but because my manager had decided I wasn't good enough to lead the team. Imagine being off work for three months to be by your husband's side as his carer, to put everything on hold to ensure he survives and come back to work – only to have that happen.

I promised myself that even when I went back to work, I wouldn't be selfish, that I would put all my attention and energy into Robert where I could. But the individual who sat in my role, who I trusted to look after my team and business during this time, stabbed me in the back for the sake of their own success.

Every day I walked into the office – my office – I would see this colleague. I would see them working their magic to convince everyone that he was leading this team better than I had ever done. That he was improving the business beyond my abilities and that my results that were now being realised, he was now claiming them as his own.

The pressure of watching this go on, working on low-value, sometimes meaningless, projects was so far short of what I could do. What I had realised was that I hadn't built a network around me. I hadn't had the time under my new manager, with my new peers, to establish a rapport so that they had my back when I was away. There was only one person that was being my sponsor that would stand up for me, but I hadn't been there to defend myself and so my reputation was being destroyed.

It was a terrible time for me. I didn't know who to trust, and my manager was so distant instead of offering support. There were times where I felt that he was just keeping me around so as to not victimise me or to lead me to make a claim of victimisation because of what Robert had gone through.

Many times, I wanted to resign and throw it all in. I was very lucky that my human resources manager, who was a supporter of mine, had my back and would guide me back to what was important in life. This wasn't important, this team, was a like a disease at times. I didn't catch the disease, but it was raising its ugly head and making me so sick and sad inside that I didn't know if I wanted to be part of this system anymore.

There was something inside of me that said, 'Don't be a quitter. Maybe quit this team, maybe seek out other opportunities, but don't quit, don't walk away, don't let them get the better of you.' So, I started to use my contacts to see what else was out in the big world. I met with several leaders within the company I worked for. I considered several roles, even ones that would see me take a step back down the corporate ladder, but nothing really captured my interest. I couldn't understand why my reputation had gone from being one of the leading young executives to now no one having faith in my capabilities.

The final heartbreaking feedback came at the end of the financial year. I had been back at work for four months and it was time to assess my year. I was honest with my manager. I felt that the first four months until I went on leave, I had implemented several great initiatives, led change and the data showed over the last three months I was away, that my efforts had showed improvement. But again, my colleague had claimed it as the result of their work. I, however, was told that I had been over-promoted and hadn't contributed like he had to the business and my work wasn't up to standard. I would never be going back to my previous role ever again.

What a kick in the teeth. My heart sank, my confidence was knocked and my ability to ever believe that I was going to be able to gain a real role in this company was over. The only people I had on my side didn't have the influence to do anything about it. I had two ways of dealing with this, either flight or fight and I chose fight. Not fight out loud, but fight to reaffirm to everyone, but mostly to myself, that

I deserved to have a role here and they would have to open the door and push me out if that's what they wanted! Because I wasn't walking.

Then, an opportunity came up to be part of a bid team to win new work with a cross-business group to bring significant revenue into the company, as well as retain jobs for our current employees. I had never done anything like this before, but I had run contracts and managed suppliers and there were lots of people around me that would help and give me guidance. I put my hand up for the position and my boss said yes. He was giving me the opportunity to either sink or swim. The only thing I wanted to do was swim.

Although the work was challenging, the people were fun to work with. They trusted me, came to me for guidance, ran ideas past me and I was a key lead on several executive calls. This was rebuilding my confidence, enabling me to learn new skills, but also prove to the non-believers, that I could rebound from their inability to support me. You don't knock down a girl from the West as she will shine through.

Lo and behold, six months later, as I worked over Christmas whilst visiting family in Melbourne when I should have been on leave, we won the contract. We were going to bring in revenues to a business that had never seen this much revenue before and keep jobs for around 700 employees.

I couldn't have been happier – and so was everyone around me. The confidence I needed to bounce back and own something that gave me purpose at work had happened. Overall, it did mean the real hard work started now, but I had the opportunity to build a new team, with new skills and prove that I was worthy of a seat at this teams table!

But then the real win came, and I was stunned by what was said to me. After going through the last nine months rebuilding my confidence, fighting for my brand and proving my capability, my boss told me that he had been wrong about me. That he had misrepresented me to his boss, the COO, and said he was sorry that he had given me such a hard time during that period.

I was so shocked as I didn't expect him to ever recognise this, much less express it to me. He was a hard man, and for him to look beyond the lies, I couldn't believe it. The reasons behind why he came to this conclusion was not just what I had just done, which was to win this amazing contract that no one thought we would, but also the performance of my colleague started to fall short.

All the work that I had done, that he had moved away from had caused the business to go backwards. It took nine months for all of this to come to light, but I felt relieved and proud that I had stuck to my guns, that I hadn't walked away and I had continued to believe in myself.

Then, my boss surprised me a second time whilst we were on a leadership retreat. With the same group of peers, we were asked to do a high ropes course. One person would climb up a tall pole and walk along a plank. The only way of not falling off was by trusting that your peers who held the ropes were not going to let you fall. The purpose of the course was to encourage everyone to have each other's back. I was laughing inside because I just didn't trust some of these guys.

Once it had been demonstrated, the instructors asked for the first volunteer. I looked around the group and decided to put my hand up. Why not, this would be a test for them and me and I would be able to prove that I could be the example for all to follow.

I got up on the pole and tentatively walked across the beam, approximately seven metres up in the air. I then walked back. I did it again, and on the last attempt the instructor asked me to run it, which

I did, both back and forth. I was so excited that I had conquered this first. That I had set the example and now the team would be able to follow in my footsteps.

When I got down from the pole, my boss walked over to me and said, 'Well done. I wouldn't have believed that you would put your hand up first. That you would lead the team by example. I am proud of you, Suzanne.' I was shocked. What I had done was build such a good rapport with my boss. It really changed how we worked with each other, and for the next year until he left the company, we had a great working relationship.

Although we had a good couple of days, we did experience some very tense moments. One of the most aggressive and egotistical managers in our team walked out because he didn't believe in what the consultants were doing – he was very rude in fact. For the most part, however, the team seemed to be working better together.

It wasn't long, once we were back at work, before tension resurfaced among the team. The pressures of what we were doing and having to drive were getting to some of them. My boss had my back, which was great, but others didn't.

We were at a peer team meeting in Melbourne three months later, when the work I was leading and the customer we were supplying to was very unhappy about our performance. I couldn't believe this was happening again. Whenever I seemed to be going well, a crisis would happen.

I was walking in and out of the room addressing the issues when one of my peers made some gesture towards me that I didn't like. He didn't feel I was representing us right and told me that he could do it better in front of my boss and peers. Between my boss and the consultants, they calmed the situation down. But he kept nit-picking at everything I said and did. I didn't react, as I wanted to see who would stand up for me and responded back politely when I didn't like what he said.

When it came to giving feedback about our managers, how they would be rated for their end of year performance, he didn't like what I said about one of his team. He told me I was being too harsh, but others in the team agreed with the examples I was giving. It had nothing to do with this manager personally, but they had dropped the ball and their focus was elsewhere. The performance had dropped and a few of their team had come to me telling me they were unhappy working for them.

Instead of representing the feedback from him, he then told his manager that I had a grudge against them because I used to lead that team and that the management team always agreed with me and never took it upon themselves to be stand up to me.

What a bloody cop-out. The manager concerned then had a go at me and didn't speak to me for months. I told them, that their manager, who I had had the run in with was weak and couldn't manage his team. It was just a ridiculous situation, with a very weak manager. When my colleague left the business, and I had to attend their farewell, I basically didn't speak to them. When they said goodbye, they told me they would like to catch up sometime. I said we would probably never be in the same circle, so good luck with whatever the future holds.

There was no way I was going to forgive him for the multiple occasions on which he was rude to me. I had liked him from the moment we first started working together despite others telling me not to trust him. Then his true colours came out and proved why he wasn't to be trusted.

I learnt so much about myself and about others throughout these years – about how to genuinely lead people and ensure you stood up for yourself. I could've written about so many other events that occurred over the years. It made me realise that in the corporate world, the only person you sometimes need to worry about is you. That events like these provide you with learnings about who you want to be and who you don't want to be.

These events, with the added pressure of Robert's diagnosis and treatment, would take a heavy toll on me. It started to accelerate my anxiety and burned me out. It took a lot of chats with Robert to realise that I couldn't keep trying to fight some of the boys and to just do my job to the best of my ability. Something had to be dropped and fighting the boys' club was it.

When we went through the next restructure, I was gifted a new team of peers who didn't work against each other. Were they perfect? No, but they were better than the previous crew. I had an opportunity to shine again, and that I did.

Over the years since I left the company, there have been many changes. Whilst I haven't spoken to the people who kicked me in the teeth, told lies about me and took my work as theirs, I have been told from my network of supporters that these people are gone. Not because they resigned, but because they were found out, displaced, and told they weren't the right fit for where the company was going.

When I heard this feedback, all I could do was smile. I don't want to be a hater, but the bullying, harassment, and transparency of how these people treated others has finally come to light. What goes around comes around, and finally the employees who worked for these selfish managers, can hopefully progress with the right leaders in place to enjoy their jobs again.

My Lesson for You:

- Engage a mentor, coach and sponsors for guidance on how to manage the politics and egos in the workplace.
- With the support and coaching of your mentor, gain confidence to speak up.
- Work hard to believe in yourself.
- Reassure yourself that the results you are delivering reflect your hard work.
- Gauge feedback from your teams, peers and managers about how you are performing. Ask them how you are going and what they think.
- Ask where you can improve and what more you can do. Always make sure you are getting a range of feedback. Work with your mentor on what you can learn or ignore from the feedback.

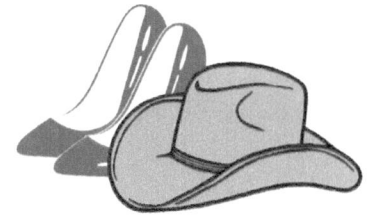

Chapter 7

Losing the Passion

In 2018, I took on another role leading a field group that installed a different type of infrastructure. I had been given the role because my boss wanted me to fix the performance, fix the team and lift the company's confidence about what we did. It took a lot of long hours for me to understand the work, the performance indicators, and the team. I made some changes and brought in a female team member to change the gender mix.

The team started to lift its performance and I was given some great feedback. I was doing my job, but something was different. In 2017, Robert had relapsed, and he relapsed for a second time in 2018. I was taking time off when he was in hospital, but everything I did at work was an effort and at times I was yelling at the team for not delivering.

Since Robert had been diagnosed with leukaemia in September 2013, and until he took voluntary redundancy in 2018, the focus was always on my career. Robert always encouraged me to strive for what I wanted in my career and he always supported me. We both knew that Robert's treatment was having an impact on his mind and body and that, at some point, allowing him to take on an easier job, something he would enjoy and predominantly outdoors would be a better outcome for him.

The company we had worked for had been very generous over the six years Robert had leukaemia. They always supported me, allowing me the leave I needed to be with Robert and or to work flexibly to be able to take him to his appointments.

Having a husband with a life-threatening disease meant that my lens on work was slowly dimming. It wasn't a rapid change, but my tolerance for anyone that whinged about the smallest things would grate on me. I would get impatient and did not want to hear about it. I continually had to hold my tongue when long-winded meetings took place. I had to try hard to concentrate when I got distracted and lost my train of thought.

In April 2019, Robert took a turn for the worse and I immediately went on leave. I thought I would only be on leave for a few days, maybe a week. But when he continued to go downhill and nearly died during the Easter of 2019, I went on leave indefinitely.

Over the next six weeks, Robert's condition was like a rollercoaster. Some days, he would be back on track with gaining strength and starting chemotherapy again, then take a nosedive due to infections and reactions to the medications and treatment.

On the 3rd of June, whilst in hospital and after several setbacks, Robert lost his ability to fight. He woke up from his induced coma to say he loved me and said goodbye – these were the last words I heard from Robert.

Robert was transferred to palliative care the next day. The doctors told me he had stopped fighting, that all his observations were now normal which was a result of him letting the disease take his life. Work was not part of my thinking. My heart was breaking, and I was in so much pain.

On the 10th of June at 5:30 am, I woke to hear Robert's second-to-last breath. As I jumped out of bed and watched the love of my life lie completely still in front of the nurse and I, he gave his last breath and his time on this earth was over.

The pain I felt in that moment and on that day was like nothing I can describe. The love of my life was gone forever. He would never speak, listen or be with me again. I was lost and empty and my whole world had changed.

Over the following three months after Robert's death, I had a lot of time to think about what work really meant to me. How was I going to go back after such a long period off? The biggest question was, did I want to?

During this time, I could not bring myself to go back to work. I led a large group of employees that ran construction teams, liaising with contractors, other executives in the company and dealing with customers. Many of the decisions we had to make to satisfy our customers were straightforward and I was starting to reflect on previous meetings and discussions, assessing whether I wanted to continue to do this.

Those last five months of hospital rooms and grieving for my husband made me realise that I had changed. I found that I had become very practised at making decisions quickly. Making the decisions that I had to in the hospital, about whether to take Robert to ICU, resuscitation and stopping treatment, all had to be made quickly and rationally. At work, decisions would take weeks, sometimes months, and I did not know how I was going to cope with this.

I also had to decide whether I wanted to go back to a desk job for the most part, and how I was going to fit travel in. In December 2018, Robert and I had moved two hours north of Brisbane. We had done it to allow Robert and I to fulfil our dream of having acreage and a farm stay business. It was also so Robert could live in the fresh air, away from the germs of the city. But now that Robert had died, I was living there by myself.

Did I want to deal with employees and their problems? Did I have enough left in me to give to others or was I spent. Was I at the point that I did not need others to depend on me, to depend on my knowledge, my advice, my care?

In August 2019, I met with my manager, who was the COO that had appointed me to my first director role in 2012. We went out to dinner in Brisbane and I told him how I was feeling – that I hadn't decided yet but would take some more time and come back to him soon on what I was going to do.

At that point, he had told me to take my time, and there was no rush to decide. The company would support me with whatever I decided to do. If I came back, they would create a role for me that worked best for me and allowed me to work from home. This all sounded great – they had my back and I had time to make the right decision.

After many conversations with family and friends, I concluded that I would resign. The life I needed to build for my future, for the person I was evolving into, wasn't fit to continue in her executive role. I knew in my heart, that leaving was easier than staying and for the first time

LOSING THE PASSION

in my life I had to do what was right for me. If I couldn't walk back into the building and lead the way I used to do with passion and conviction, then my time as an executive was over.

In September 2019, I rang and told my manager that I was resigning. He was not surprised and thought when we met in August that this might have been my decision. He was happy that I had thoroughly thought it through from a personal, financial, and business point of view and knew I hadn't made the decision lightly.

I told him that I was not the person my people used to know and did not have the energy to give them or the business what they needed. I knew a lot of my current and past teams and colleagues would be upset to see me go. But they also saw some of the toll the last few years had taken on me and knew that if I said I couldn't do this anymore than it would have been a rational and calculated decision to call it a day.

Then came the day to make it official. I dialled into a team meeting that my peers and direct reports had been asked to join. My manager gave them the news and provided me with a wonderful wrap on all that I had achieved over the 25 years of working for this company. It gave me a chance to thank everyone for their support, their messages over the last five months and what had enabled me to come to this decision.

The company put on one last dinner for me in October, to which I just invited my close team members. I did not want the big fanfare. I was not leaving because I was off to some new job. I was leaving because I had changed, my life had changed, and it was time to find myself a new purpose for the future.

I could not have been any more grateful for the managers and staff that had assisted, supported and cared for me over the last six years. I walked away from an amazing caring company, with skills, knowledge and achievements that I would have never thought was possible when I started 25 years ago.

But more importantly, I walked away with pride in knowing that I choose to end an amazing career, and with several amazing friendships that I will have for the rest of my life. As I stood on my patio and looked out across the rolling mountains, I would always be thankful for what I have. I would always know this company allowed me to have everything I needed for the future, but now it was all about ME!

My Lesson for You:

- If you do not like the role you are currently in, find a new job.
- If your role isn't satisfying you, find a new job.
- If the person or company you are working for makes you feel uncomfortable, find a new job.
- Don't let anyone tell you there isn't a new job out there for you. The job is there, but it just might take some time to find it.
- Never settle for average in a job. You deserve to work in a role that motivates you, brings out your passion and is aligned to your values.

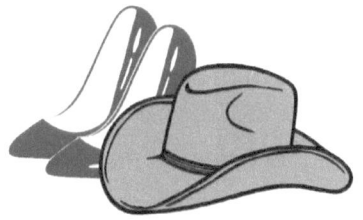

Chapter 8

A Country Girl at Heart

I was very grateful to have grown up with loving, supportive parents who always took us on regular adventures. I had several family members and some of my parents' friends that lived on property or had horses. We were always going away camping – staying in tents or caravans was the norm.

I was always bought up as being equal to my cousins and friends. I had girl and boy friends. We played in the paddocks behind our house, rode our bikes to the creek to collect tadpoles, I played cricket and football with the boys and getting dirty didn't worry me.

During my childhood, we would always take the six-hour trip north from Melbourne to Mildura, at the top of Victoria, during holidays to visit my great Auntie Ivy and Uncle Clarrie at Easter and Christmas.

They lived on 10 acres and my uncle was a dairy farmer in his day. Their property was situated in the middle of thousands of grapevines

– Mildura is the Victorian capital of wine in my eyes – and my uncle agisted harness racehorses in his paddock.

Every time my brother and I went to their place, we would roam the paddocks, take hay out of my uncle's shed, entice the horses into the stalls and I would feed and pat them for hours on end.

My uncle had chickens and we loved chasing them around the house. One day my brother, Paul, chased one of my uncle's prized chooks under the house – although he tells me now that it wasn't him, it was our cousin, I am still not convinced! Mildura is always hot, and my uncle was so mad that maybe a snake would bite it or the chicken would die under there. We were all yelled at and told never to do it again. I feared him that day!

They also had a large vegetable garden full of tomatoes, pumpkin, corn, lettuce and cabbage. I remember my brother eating some of the best tomatoes off the vine, and we were never allowed to kick the football or play cricket near it just in case we damaged the crops. No wonder our uncle yelled at us frequently.

We were always out helping my uncle with his produce, and we often skipped over the fence and the irrigation channels to grab a few bunches of sweet grapes from the neighbours.

On the odd occasion, we would be warned that a snake had been in their laundry or on the patio and to be careful. They also had an outside toilet. I remember pushing the door open hard and sometimes leaving it open because I was scared that a snake or spider would suddenly appear.

Knowing this made us a little apprehensive at first, but being kids, it didn't take long to forget what we had been told and we were outside playing on the lawn or in the paddocks in 40-degree heat.

Paul and I loved the freedom we had on their property. We loved kicking around in the dirt and pretending that their property was ours!

Another uncle, Uncle Laurie, my dad's brother, owned 200 acres near Bendigo. Uncle Laurie and Auntie Thora farmed beef cattle and sheep and we visited him at least once a year.

Again, Paul and I loved to roam the property within the boundaries of the house and go exploring. He had a lush creek that ran across the front of the property. You parked your car on the other side of the creek and had to cross a walkway that was like a troll bridge to get to their house.

A few times, we had arrived and walked over the bridge and my uncle would say that the bridge had a black snake under it and we had to be careful. The snakes in Victoria are venomous, and although Paul and I were scared, it didn't stop us from running backwards and forwards over it to try and scare the snake away.

On one visit, Paul and I saw that there was a sheep in the cattle yards. We didn't know what the sheep was there for, so we decided to play with it. Well, when I say play with it, basically we chased it around in circles in the cattle yard until it nearly dropped dead.

Then my dad received a call from his brother a few days later to say the sheep had dropped dead, probably from a heart attack after we chased it around for hours, and the meat was too tough to eat from all the stress. Oh no… we were told to never do that to animals again!

The third place we used to visit which was my favourite, my Aunty Judy and Uncle Peter's (dad's cousin) place. Their daughter, Cherie, my cousin, who is older than me, had horses. Her first horse that I remember riding was a grey pony called Trixie. I loved going to their house in the hope that I would be able to ride her. Nothing made me happier than to hear that we were going to their house in Lilydale.

On the visits where we didn't ride, I would be so disappointed. I loved playing out in their large backyard and calling the horses to the fence. I was usually a bit scared as a few of Cherie's horses were quite tall, but I would stay on the wooden fence, hoping that they would walk over so I could pat them. Cherie was a great rider, competing in lots of different shows including the prestigious Garryowen Event at the Melbourne Show. I was so inspired by my cousin and her horses that I always nagged my parents to buy me one.

When I was 11 years of age, I had a couple of friends who owned horses. I remember telling my mum I was going to a friend's place to play, which I would, then we would go to the paddocks where the horses were and feed, groom and ride them.

When I was 14, I also had a friend who had a horse. She rode 15 kilometres to my house one day and we went riding through the streets. I loved catching up and riding on the back of her horse with her. On this day, we came across some guys on motorbikes. My friend's horse spooked and bucked me off. I then had to walk home whilst she had to walk the 15 kilometres to get back to her paddock. This experience didn't scare me off horses; it made me want to learn and ride even more.

As an adult, if anyone said, 'Let's go on a trail ride,' I would go. When Robert and I went to Egypt and South America, we rode donkeys and horses. Robert would always get the fast horse and he would gallop through the paddocks, where I had the old horse.

In 2016, we had the most memorable horse experience. Our 16-year-old goddaughter who loves horses came to Queensland for a week's holiday with a friend. As a surprise, we took her to a ranch south of Ballina in New South Wales and went horse-riding on the beach. Even though Robert had neuropathy in his feet and couldn't feel them, he still wanted to enjoy the experience with Abby.

The four of us took the horses onto the beach and Abby, who had the most riding experience of all of us, took her horse and surfed the waves. It has been one of the most magical rides that I have ever done, and you couldn't get the smile off our faces. We stayed at the ranch and the girls helped in the paddocks. It was a special time, and I am so grateful that we made those memories with her and Robert.

The only horse I ever owned was my Barbie Horse, Dallas! I loved playing with Western Barbie, Western Ken and Dallas. I had the 4x4 Western Truck that pulled the horse float, and I would take them out into the backyard and play with them for hours on end. I dreamed that one day I would have horses and floats and ride them in my own backyard. I would draw horses and watch every horse show that was on TV or at the movies. My cousin had given me a love of horses that I would always treasure, and it was always my dream that one day I would bring it to life.

During my childhood, I always had a love of country and farm life. My family had fostered it from a very young age and as I moved into my adult years, there was always a thought there that someday I would have acreage myself.

I don't remember the first day Robert and I discussed it, but it must have been early on in our relationship that we wanted to set up a bed and breakfast at some stage. When we went to the United Kingdom in 1998, we hired a car and drove around England, Scotland and Wales and stayed at country inns and B&Bs. I loved the homeliness of these places, most of the people who owned them were so nice, happy and loved to have a chat. Robert and I talked about doing the same in Australia. We could have a bed and breakfast as a farm stay one day to welcome people into our home and show them our lifestyle.

We loved taking trips with our friends, hiring houses or staying in cabins. We stayed in Healesville in three cabins spread apart with friends on long weekends. We would visit the local town or markets and then settle in for an afternoon of enjoying local produce and wine.

Every time Robert and I went to these places for long weekends after we moved to Queensland in 2009, we started to think seriously about what our dream business would look like. We had to have acreage, preferably cabins, so that we could separate the guests from our home. We would provide the guests with local treats, big Saturday night dinners around a campfire and a few animals that our guests and their kids could feed.

We had a vision of what it could look like. We didn't talk about it often, but we knew what we were working towards for our future. Paying off our house and working hard were all leading up to one day living our dream.

When Robert was diagnosed with leukaemia in 2013 and after he had a bone marrow transplant in 2014, our dream became a topic that was discussed regularly. We met a couple that lived in the Mary Valley, two hours north of Brisbane in the hospital. He had had a bone marrow transplant the same time as Robert and he and his wife lived on 150 acres.

Our first long weekend at their house was breathtaking. Their property was nestled on the edge of a state forest. They had horses, cows, and chickens. Robert would ride around on the quad bike whilst I would meander around the vegie patch, gardens, and paddocks. In our eyes, they were living the life we both wanted, and the more we visited their property, the more we wanted to spend our lives in this beautiful part of the world.

In 2018, after Robert had relapsed, he decided it was time to start looking for a property and make this dream a reality.

Over a four-week period, Robert would go up to the Sunshine Coast hinterlands and inspect a range of acreage or properties to find the one that would fulfil our dreams. We sought advice on whether we should buy land and build or find a property with an existing house, infrastructure, and sheds. Then, we sat down with our friends who lived in the area to show them the properties that we were thinking of inspecting.

Robert and I agreed that it would be better for us to buy a property that already had a house on it. Having the utilities and infrastructure in place, along with a dam and sheds, was a better option. When we were looking through the properties, one that I thought was out of price range took our eye. I had been looking at it for six months but didn't think we could afford. After some discussion we made the decision to visit the town of Kenilworth the next day and check out the property from the road.

Kenilworth is a beautiful town with a pub, post office, grocer, pharmacy, doctor and a very famous bakery. When we arrived on the Sunday, the town was full of people, with a great atmosphere and we really liked the vibe. Plus, it was only two hours from Brisbane, so it was easily accessible for me if I was required to still commute to work.

Viewing the house from the road wasn't possible. The house was situated on a hill and although we thought we could see where it was, it was very well hidden behind bushes and trees. We made the decision that

Robert would inspect the house during the week and if he thought it was worth me looking at it, we would return the following weekend.

Robert made the drive to Coolabine to inspect the house, as I anxiously awaited his call. Because Robert was in remission, he was so damn excited about the possibility of moving there. Before he could drive out of the driveway, he was on the phone telling me he had booked a second inspection for the Saturday. He described all the amazing features of the house, the acreage, and the magnificent views, and told me I would fall in love with it.

Well, he wasn't wrong. When we arrived on the Saturday, drove up the steep driveway and saw the house for the first time, it took my breath away. As we stepped out of the car and looked beyond the house to the views of the valley, I felt like I was home. Once we had inspected the house, which blew my mind, and the sheds out the back, the owner took us for a drive around the paddocks. I was in love.

I couldn't believe that this might be our dream house and property. Before we said goodbye to the agent and the owner, we told them that we would look at our numbers. We were interested and we would come back to them with an offer within the week.

We jumped back in the car, trying to control our excitement, but by the time we hit the road and drove beyond the gates, we were on such a high. Robert was totally in love; he was telling me everything we could do to the place. Cabins could be built on the ridge beyond the sheds. He told me about how we could turn one of the sheds into the office, where the car parking could go, where the pool was going to be built and where my horses could go!

'What, horses? I can have horses too?' I asked him excitedly. He said, 'Why not? It has always been your dream, so you can have a horse too!' Oh my god! I was thinking, we are going to do this, we are going to make an offer, we are going to bring forward our dream of living in the country and setting up our B&B business.

Over the next few weeks, we secured a loan and bought the house. However, we didn't move in after the settlement date as Robert had relapsed in June and needed to have more chemotherapy in hospital. We were lucky that the owner wasn't ready to move out either, so he stayed in the house for a few extra months until we were both in agreement to make the move.

I still can't believe today that we had fast-tracked our dream. That Robert's leukaemia diagnosis, bone marrow transplant and then a relapse had changed our thinking that life was too short to hold on to a dream for another 10 years. Now was the time, and Robert wanted to start living a stress-free life in nature and be outdoors.

Of course, all I wanted was to fulfil the dream too. But I also wanted to do it with a healthy, happy, and leukaemia-free husband.

This may not be a surprise to my family and friends, but in 2017, on the way back from a trip to Broome, I had already developed a spreadsheet and business plan to kick off my dream. At the time, I didn't know when it would happen, but I was already mentoring a friend who had started her first business, and she suggested I should also start doing mine. The great thing about the plan was it helped me to get through the hard times with work and Robert's diagnosis. Something to plan for that filled my heart with joy.

In November 2018, we took over the property, moved small pieces of furniture in and spent every weekend up in Coolabine. Then, in the middle of December, after selling our house in Brisbane, we permanently moved.

We left our city life and all that we had made of it behind. Our house and lifestyle in Brisbane were amazing, but there were also many challenging times throughout Robert's diagnosis. I didn't know until then that Robert had some bad memories still floating in his consciousness from unhappy times during his illness. He told me that one of his driving forces for the move was to have a new start, a new life, one that would be stress-free in the country.

I couldn't agree with him more. We had so much to look forward to. So much to learn, so much to grow, so much to build. We were entering the third chapter of our life together. We had moved from Melbourne to Brisbane after 10 years of marriage to fulfil my career.

Now, after 10 years in Brisbane we were moving to Coolabine, to fulfil our dream. Life seemed amazing.

In some ways, and I know this may sound strange, in that moment I was grateful for what we had learnt from Robert's diagnosis. If we had our time again, we wouldn't wish it upon ourselves, but it did teach us that life is on borrowed time. Where there is a will there is a way. That anyone can fulfil their dreams with a bit of hard work, commitment and passion.

We didn't know what the future held for Robert or for me. I had the flexibility in my executive role to be able to work from different locations and although we had to go back to Brisbane twice a week for Robert's treatment, we would balance our weekdays to make it work!

As we awoke to the view of the mountains outside our bedroom window on the first morning of living there, and the fresh air started to fill our lungs, we knew together we had made the best decision of our lives. We had listened to our gut instincts and was going to make our dream a reality. I loved this man who loved to take risks and was able to visualise our future.

Together, we were so much more in love with life than we could have ever dreamed of!

My Lesson for You:

- Your dream will always be a dream if you don't work on it.
- You can balance your job and your life by creating your dream.
- Start off by developing a business plan. You can find them on the Government's small business websites. They are a great template to get you started.
- Start mapping out a timeline. How long do you need to develop your dream, how much money, what can you do now?
- Start talking about your dream, but most importantly what you are doing to create it. No one likes hearing, 'I have a dream', and that is it!
- Take the plunge. Of course, it can be risky, but if you have done your due diligence and you have the support of your loved ones, you can make your dream a reality.

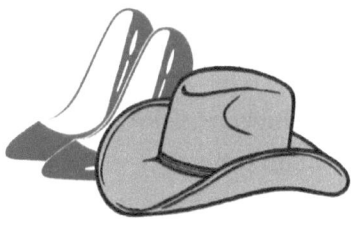

Chapter 9

Living the Country Life Alone

The first day I woke up living on 35 acres alone was in September 2019. When Robert died in June of that year, my parents stayed with me for three months. They cared for me throughout the toughest months of my life, but I had to start living independently and it was time for them to resume their life.

The day after they left, I experienced the unexpected loss of my two dogs. I had just lost my husband and now my two dogs had accidentally died from baiting. It wasn't their fault; I had let them wander while I was building a new path. I knew the baiting was starting, but I didn't realise it was that day and I allowed them to roam into the danger.

The heartache of losing those two dogs was horrendous. I had been by myself for two days and I had let this happen. The guilt was gut-wrenching and although I kept saying to myself that Robert needed those dogs more than I did, it didn't really make a huge difference. I had been negligent on day two of my new life and it had ended in tragedy.

When I returned to my house after staying at a friend's house for two nights, it was now day four of living alone. The house was even emptier – just me and my five chickens. I knew my next-door neighbours, but that was all. We hadn't met any other people in Coolabine or Kenilworth since moving in in December. Most of our time had been spent in Brisbane for Robert's treatment and meeting new people hadn't been an option.

It was also in September when I made the decision to resign from my corporate executive role. This would mean that I had ample time on my property to start thinking about what was next. I had to keep busy because if I wasn't, then my mind would be wandering, ruminating on the death of Robert or my beloved puppies.

My grief was raw – I cried a lot, but now I was starting to think that Robert had gifted me this property and he wanted me to fulfil our dreams. During the last week he was alive, I had promised him that I would build our business and live the life we had wanted together.

Robert and I had spoken about the projects that we wanted to do, so I decided that I needed to get onto them.

The first projects required clearing out some overgrown areas that we didn't like. It was, and still is, very therapeutic removing overgrown bushes, cleaning up fallen branches and clearing the ground of leaves. During September, I had my cousin and two girlfriends come up at separate times to help and it was the perfect way to get a lot done.

My cousin, Deb, who lives in Albury, came up for a week. She and I cleared and chopped down overgrown shrubs around the old pool and replanted with existing plants. We cleaned out the gutters on the sheds and laid gutter guard. We started the huge job of clearing behind the house in readiness for building a deck and replanted the herb garden.

When Denise came, we cleared out half of the garden next to the sheds. It was so densely overgrown with shrubs, and I wanted to make a path through it. I also wanted to build it up with some ground covers, bromeliads, and ferns so that when people visited, they could walk through a mini sanctuary.

Sharon arrived a few weeks later and we cleared the remainder of the side area that Denise and I had started on. We tore down old wire from the fence, planted new ferns and made a path through the entire area.

The satisfaction of doing this with the people who loved me filled my heart with joy. My beautiful friends had come up to support me by giving up their time and although my girlfriends and I were city chicks, we put our backs into it and completed these projects together.

There were several other areas that I had the pleasure of clearing – behind the house was the biggest. When Deb and I got our first glimpse of the view of the mountains behind the house, we were blown away. Right in front of us were the Conondale National Park mountains. The blue haze that sits above them most evenings was sensational, and I was so happy that Robert had suggested we clear all the bushes out to showcase the view.

In November, my gorgeous friends, John and Di, came up to continue the work Deb and I had started. Over three days we chopped down every bush that was in that area. It was a hard job in 30-degree heat. We didn't have much protection from the sun, but we were determined to complete the jobs that Robert and I had discussed to open the view and enjoy the peaceful mountains that surrounded us.

It wasn't all work, work, work during this time. I had the opportunity to do a few things that I hadn't done before. The first was to attend the annual wine and cheese festival held in Kenilworth with John and Di. Local producers of wine, foods and crafts fill the Kenilworth Dairy and adjoining park to showcase their produce. There were bands playing and a crowd of wonderful smiling locals and tourists.

I also took the opportunity to go to my first local rodeo in which is held during the local Kenilworth Show. The atmosphere, horsemanship and cowboy skills were so exciting.

The competition was fierce, and I loved the excitement of the crowd and the participants. I had a rush of blood and held my breath every time the cowgirls and boys launched themselves into the arena participating in barrel racing, bucking bulls and so much more. The emcee got the audience participation going and they played country music between competitors.

What I loved the most was the camaraderie between the competitors. Most of these women and men knew each other as they would compete in various rodeos. They would help each other if someone was hurt and of course clap their competitors or pat them on the backs after a great ride.

There were also rides for the kids, show horse competitions, showbags and fireworks at night. Country people are confronted with so many obstacles – droughts, floods, prices of stock or produce – but when they come to the local show/rodeo, all that seems to disappear, and they just love coming together.

I also took the opportunity to help some friends harvest their macadamia nuts. Twice a year they harvest their nuts, and they are always looking for people to help them. I had never seen the harvesting process operate before, so I decided to give them a hand and understand how the process worked.

For a small local producer, the process of harvesting is literally backbreaking, as macadamias are harvested from the ground. The nuts fall to the ground and a large machine sweeps them up, but they also sweep up any sticks or rocks. To ensure they don't break the sorting machines, you need to separate the nuts from the debris.

For four hours, while someone swept the nuts towards the end of the trailer, I helped to separate the nuts from the debris. Sticks and stones in one bucket, while nuts were moved onto the concrete behind us. Of course, we weren't silent while doing it – we chatted, laughed and prepared the nuts for the next part of the process, separating the good from the bad.

As we started the machine, I had my watchful eye on the nuts that came through the chute. All the broken or damaged nuts needed to be removed off the conveyor belt and only the A-class nuts were to be taken for sale. It was important to get this right, as it would impact the quality of the product, and of course the price.

I seemed to be doing a pretty good job of it and just loved learning a new skill and how the macadamia harvesting process worked. I then went into the orchard, where I saw how the machine swept the nuts off the ground, how the nuts are damaged by cockatoos and how the wild pigs loved getting through the fences for a good feed of maccas.

It was an exciting day for me, even if it was well outside of the corporate world that I was used to. Seeing the produce sitting in the trailer, waiting to go to market, was satisfying.

My friends also farm a small herd of beef cattle. You need to muster the cows into the yards to spray them, tag them and neuter the steers. Again, they needed some help doing this, and with two other friends to help them, the four of us got to work to drive the cows into the yard to be backlined/sprayed and the steers neutered.

I have never been in a small pen with 20 cows and calves, waving plastic pipe to muster them into the pens. I watched my friends carefully and then said I could do it while they did the spraying and other tasks. Some of these cows, all females, were very protective of their calves and did not like being herded into a small pen.

On a couple of occasions, they came running towards us, and we had to quickly jump out of the way or up the railings. It was like watching a Western show on TV. I loved the adrenaline that rushed through me when we herded the cows into the small yard. The fear that coursed through my veins and bones, not knowing what an aggressive cow was going to do, was exhilarating. I loved the whole process and the work it took to get this job done.

It was so rewarding to see all 25 animals sprayed, tagged and neutered before being returned to the paddock. We high-fived each other as the last cow ran into the paddock, I was so damn happy that I had contributed to their farm.

No cow or human was injured during the three-hour process. I had learnt so much around the temperament of the animal and why farmers must do these processes. Being out in the country air with a great group of people was a double bonus and I was really starting to feel that this country life, beyond my property, was exactly where I wanted to be.

The one trait I have picked up from my father, and probably his brothers, as well as Robert, is that I will give anything a go. Most of my cousins that I grew up with were boys. My family had farming in their blood and I loved the feeling at the end of the day when you could look back at what you had physically accomplished and say, 'Job well done.'

After my first couple of farmhand experiences, I was happy to help whoever needed it. It was a great way to learn new skills, have some fun and meet new people. I didn't get too much opportunity in the following year with Covid, but it gave me the appreciation of what it meant to live on and operate a small farm.

Other than doing projects and having friends visit, I have become accustomed to my own company. During the first Covid lockdown in March 2020, the six weeks that I was at home taught me to live by myself.

Chores that I took for granted when people were visiting or when Mum and Dad were up, were now all mine. I would have to cook three meals a day, as Uber Eats isn't available in the country. The only takeaway was pizza or from the pub. Although I have ordered takeaways from the pub a couple of times, 95 per cent of my meals are cooked by me.

Loneliness does creep in, and depression has clouded me at times. I have engaged the help of a psychologist to help me through those tough days and weeks. I have learnt how to be able to look down into the black hole and step away, rather than taking a step into it and losing myself to the world of grief.

It has taken plenty of strength some days to do the cleaning, washing, dishes, feed the animals and keep the property looking great. There have been periods where I haven't washed the dishes, washed my hair or rode my horses for 10 days. I am still learning how to manage my single self and allow myself slack on some days.

When I take it easy and care for myself, I sit on my patio looking out at the hills and breathe in the country air. I do a lot of reading and writing, and I am preparing the collateral for my cabins. I love naps, getting my vitamin D and I have started to do meditation. If I am lonely, I love sitting in the paddock, watching my horses with Archie, and on days when I am sad, I let the tears stream down my cheeks.

I fill in my days, when lazy days are called for, doing puzzles, cross stitch, drawing or collage. Mindfulness activities that take concentration stop me from ruminating and staring down that black hole.

I joined a life drawing group in August 2020. They are a great mix of people of different genders, generations and backgrounds who all love drawing. Every fortnight we get together in Imbil. I haven't drawn since school, but the two hours we draw I get lost in the art and I live in the moment. We have lots of laughs and chats, and I have become a part of a group that gives me joy and energy.

Grief post-Robert since living in the country has been hard. I never thought I would cope or that I could live by myself. But I have a resilience and inner strength that I have built over the years and I draw on that from the experiences and events that I have gone through.

I have become quite spiritual and believe in the universe delivering good people to me. Living by myself has made me more appreciative of family, friends and people I love and who care for me.

I have also become tougher and have learnt to hold my own. At times I haven't been the most wonderful friend and although not an excuse, being judged and criticised has seen me react in not-so-wonderful ways. Grief sometimes can appear with ugliness. It's not always tears – it can be anger, and sometimes people have been offended by what I have said and done. But the friends that have stepped away, I thank them for the time they spent with me. Not everyone will be friends forever and I am always happy for new friends to come my way.

I do have wonderful neighbours and one who is a very dear friend now and when she hasn't seen me for days, she messages me asking if I am OK. That makes a huge difference because the people you think that would check up on you don't, and that is what brings in the loneliness.

During Covid in 2020 and 2021, I have only had three months where my parents, god-daughters and old neighbours have visited from Melbourne. I live for those visits. Being able to spoil my friends, showcase my beautiful property and engage in conversation makes my life complete.

I also have an amazing friendship group that live in Brisbane; too many to name. At different times they come to see me, and I go to see them. We go on holidays, have girls' weekends and enjoy life. They always warm my heart. I am so grateful that I have made those friends, as life would be lonely without them!

Country life is teaching me new skills, values, behaviours and dreams. I am starting to discover who I am as a widowed woman and that is something I will continue to learn. Everything I have done so far; I have no regrets. It is making me a more independent woman with more passion and motivation to realise my dream!

My Lesson for You:

- Embrace the people that want to be in your life – they are the ones that will get you through the tough times.
- Try new experiences. You will be surprised how much fun you may have just by giving something a go.
- Write down what you are passionate about or something you have always wanted to do and do it. Be part of a new group and embrace your passion.
- Even when you don't want to go out, go out. Once you get there, I am sure you will be grateful for being around people that love you.
- Drink lots of water and eat good food. When you are living by yourself, you need to be fit and healthy.

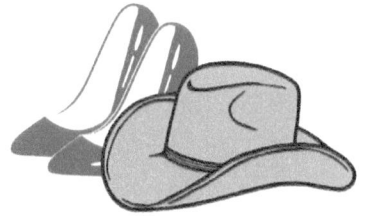

Chapter 10

The Power of Animals

Some of my first memories as a child involved animals. My first dog was a beagle called Sandy and first cat was Snowball. We had fish and budgies growing up too, and I remember my brother having a guinea pig.

Robert and I had two dogs when we first got married – Bodhi, a Pomeranian cross fox terrier and Jackson, a brown Labrador. They lived until they were aged 16 and 14, respectively. They were two peas in a pod, always hanging around together, sleeping together, playing together and eating together. When Bodhi died after what we suspect was a stroke, Jackson continued to live for another two years by himself. Although he was very lonely without his mate, he was such a loving and loyal boy.

At the end of 2016, after Robert was diagnosed with leukaemia and had his bone marrow transplant, we decided to get a Jack Russell cross poodle named Jonty. He was a funny little fellow. He jumped a metre high when he saw anyone for the first time.

He was full of love and fun and he was the first dog we let sleep in our room at night.

Jonty would be Robert's little mate during the day when Robert was on sick leave after he relapsed and I was at work. He would comfort Robert after he came home from his treatments. Robert would fall asleep on the lounge most afternoons and Jonty would jump up and sleep on or beside Robert. Jonty knew when Robert needed extra love and was not himself and was always there to give Robert hugs.

On afternoons where Robert would go to our bedroom for a long nap, I would find Jonty curled up beside him on the bed cuddling and keeping him company. I loved the way Jonty would decide who needed his love most at night. Most of the time due to Robert's illness it was him. But on the odd occasion and especially after Robert went to bed, he would turn his attention to me.

When I was out running or walking, Jonty would come with me. He loved getting out on the pavement with me and he could run forever. When we were training to hike the overland track in Tasmania in 2017, Jonty at five months walked the 10 kilometres that we hiked through the forest. He ran and ran with our friends two dogs. He did around 20 kilometres that day. Running with them and then back to us, back and forth for most of the trip. He was in doggie heaven.

If I was working from home, I would bring his bed into our office and he would lay there, mostly sleeping and keeping a watchful eye on me. Everyone in my team knew Jonty, and on the odd occasion he would be registered as attending a meeting because he had been sitting on my lap for most of it. He was a faithful dog with a heart of gold.

When we moved to Coolabine in December 2018, I decided to buy a second dog to keep Jonty occupied on the property. I had always wanted a border collie, but Robert did not want to buy one until we had acreage. So, on the day after we moved, Harry joined our family. He was a short-haired collie – black and white and always had a big smile on his face.

Jonty and Harry became inseparable. They loved roaming the paddocks and going on little adventures together. I would take them out on the dirt roads for a walk. Sometimes they would go into the paddocks and chase the cows. Jonty was always in front, the leader of the two while Harry was content to follow and run around with his best mate.

After spending two months away from them, and after Robert died, these two dogs were my everything for the next three months. They would sleep with me in the bedroom, sometimes up on the bed. They would comfort me on the couch at night, Harry beside me and Jonty on my lap. I would take them to friends' houses for dinner. They would continue to come on hikes in the local forest. Anywhere I would go, they would come with me.

It was in the September of 2019, when they both accidently ate poisoned bait that had been laid for the wild dogs (through a controlled legal program run by the local council with local farmers), that my world fell apart. These two dogs had comforted me through the worst nights of my life. That had given me light every morning when they jumped up on my bed to say 'hello' with their big smiles and lots of love. Now, they were gone from my life and left another big hole in my heart. In some ways, losing them so unexpectedly was as devastating as losing Robert.

After losing Robert in June 2019 and then the dogs in September, the only animals I had with me were five chickens. Now I think my chickens are quite unique. They love to receive pats and when I crouch down beside them, they will squat waiting for me to massage them. They love what I call their chook massages and are not afraid to jump up to me, especially when I have food! But they were chickens, and they didn't keep me warm and loved at night.

After a lonely three months, I made the decision to buy my next buddy, the canine love of my life, Archie. Archie was an unexpected find. I was at my best friend's house in Melbourne, searching for a dog on the internet for them to adopt as a pet. We were finding it hard to find one for their family, so I decided to look for short-haired border collies in QLD/NSW.

As I was scrolling through the pages on Gumtree, I found a first-time breeder of working dogs, the breed I wanted, border collie cross kelpie for sale. They had two puppies left, both males, which was what I was looking for. I kept looking at the pictures, reading the descriptions, discussing with my bestie and her family saying, 'Should I, shouldn't I?' Then they said, 'Why don't you just enquire and see if they have any left?'

When I enquired, they said they only had one left. His face was so cute and I really wanted to buy him, but I was going to Bali in two days. The dog was in NSW near Ballina/Byron Bay and I wouldn't be able to pick him up for another week. The ruminating got the best of me and I decided if they would hold him until I got back from Bali in a week's time, then I would buy him. Thankfully, they did and I became the owner of my new dog!

On the day I got back from Bali, in lieu of driving north home from Brisbane Airport, I took the trek south over the border and met my new mate, Archie. He was all legs and his mum and dad had great temperaments. I was in love from the moment I laid eyes on him and together we took the four-hour drive back north to his new home.

From the first night, Archie was a special dog. He was already basically toilet trained at 12 weeks. He jumped around and followed me everywhere. He snuggled up on the couch with me and I could tell he would have me breaking all my previous rules between a dog and their owner. He was another dog that had a sense of what I needed. He would melt my heart and heal it all at the same time.

Archie is such a loyal boy. When my parents or friends come to visit, he will want attention and pats from them. But if I move inside or walk away, he is always right beside me. He has been my confidante during the hard times. He has been my box of tissues through the sad times. He is always looking out for me and is a loyal guard dog, protecting me and our house.

He does tend to want to herd the cattle which has caused some frustration with the neighbours at times. But he isn't doing that as much these days after some professional training and, overall, he is just doing what his natural instincts tell him.

Many a time when I have been at my worst and contemplated horrible thoughts during the night, I have brought Archie inside and he has jumped up on the bed. He lays beside me, putting his paw on my chest and snuggling his head into my neck. If I didn't have him some nights, I don't know what would've happened. He always knows when I need his love, his comfort and his trust.

I don't go many places without my best mate. He always comes into town with me. He has come with me to friends' houses for dinner, gone on overnighters to my friends in Brisbane and even come camping with me to Coolum for a couple of nights.

I remember taking Archie to a friend's house in Brisbane. Rob had had a bone transplant with Robert and we had become great friends. After Robert died, Rob relapsed. I took Archie to their house; he was just a puppy and had only had him less than two weeks. After exploring the kitchen and loungeroom, we all sat down on the couch and Archie laid under Rob's legs.

It was the most amazing thing to watch. Sometimes you wouldn't believe these moments unless you see them yourself. Archie didn't give any attention to Claire or I – just Rob. For the next hour, he slept peacefully between Rob's feet. We all said he must have known that Rob needed Archies love more than anyone else. I realised that day that I had bought such a special dog!

The more time that passes, the more connected Archie and I have become. He follows me around the farm, comes riding with me in the paddocks and comes to lunch in town. He barks at the snakes, foxes and any visitors when they come to the house. But deep down he has a heart of gold and I always tell him I love him every night and give him a kiss before bed.

As mentioned previously, I have always had a love of horses. After Robert died in 2019, I decided that I wanted to fulfil the dream of being able to own a horse and learn to ride properly.

In November 2019, I had my first horse-riding lesson. I thought I was better than I was and had a big reality check during this lesson! Yes, I could walk a horse and hold onto the saddle tight when trotting and cantering, but I was rubbish at steering and riding!

I started to take fortnightly lessons from my wonderful horse-riding instructor. The other reason for the lessons is that I had booked a horse-riding tour in Patagonia, South America in March 2020. The ride was for five days, and I needed to be able to ride for four days through the picturesque mountains of Argentina.

I would always get to my half an hour lesson early to watch the client before me. I always patted the horses in the paddock on the way in. Then as I got more confident, started to help unsaddle and groom the horses post my lesson, and take them back to their paddocks.

Horse-riding lessons were the best part of my weeks. I was learning a lot of basic skills that would build my confidence over the first four months. I loved my instructor; she had a beautiful calm nature and treated her horses with such care and love. I would ride three different horses during my time there, depending on what she wanted to teach me. Each horse had such a wonderful nature, and I quickly built my confidence around these magnificent animals.

THE POWER OF ANIMALS

In the lead-up to the trip, I leased a horse that I put on a friend's property for four weeks. Her name was Charmaine, a grey mare with a little bit of attitude. A nearby horse-riding/trail-riding school enabled you to lease them for a month at a time. This would enable me to further build my confidence and skills in the lead up to our trip.

Twice a week, I would go and ride Charmaine. She was a bit challenging as she was a pack horse and didn't like being ridden away from the other horses on the property. I would take her out the back of their property, practising my trotting and holding on to the saddle to canter and gallop. At this point I also needed to strengthen my muscles as long days in a saddle can give you a real work out!

What I loved about leasing Charmaine was that I had to care for her: I had to groom her, take care of her hooves, and build a relationship with her so that I could reduce the fear I sometimes felt. I just wanted to ride with the wind in my hair. But I would come to realise once I owned my own horses that it was necessary to build a relationship between you and your horse, and riding was the outcome from that.

Charmaine challenged me when I was riding her, and although I never fell off, we did have a few times where I would have to dismount and try and take her through obstacles that she didn't want to tackle. Sometimes she would shy and not want to do what I was asking her to do. I had to be calm as I was riding her by myself. But this would also upset me, because I couldn't see myself getting to the stage where I would be confident enough to have my own animals.

A week before our trip, I had to say goodbye to Charmaine, but my instructor said she could see the progress I had made in my riding by having her. I noticed at my lessons that my strength in my core and thighs was starting to improve and sitting in the saddle seemed more natural. Even though I didn't get to where I wanted to, it had improved my riding strength and some mental alertness to how horses can react.

Unfortunately, Covid hit. My trip to South America was cancelled and my horse-riding lessons had to stop. I really missed not going to my lessons, which were now on a weekly basis. I missed being around these amazing animals and how much energy I got from them.

Instead of riding, I started to watch horse-riding videos of reputable horse people. I loved the way they worked with their horses and the horses with them. I started to understand how important the relationship between the two was and gained more knowledge of how to build that relationship.

In June 2020, I returned to my horse-riding lessons. I felt like my confidence had reduced, which was to be expected as I hadn't been around or ridden a horse for three months. But after getting my first taste of horsemanship and watching all those videos, I really wanted to take this seriously and had decided when the opportunity arose, I wanted to buy a horse.

In August 2020, due to unforeseen circumstances, my horse-riding instructor needed to lease out a few of her horses. Covid had hit her business hard, and she needed to find homes for a few of them. Of course, I jumped at the opportunity to lease two horses indefinitely. This was going to be another dream that would be fulfilled, and I couldn't wait to have them at my house.

On one sunny day in August, Chant and Minty arrived at my property in their rugs and halters ready to experience life at Coolabine Retreat.

For the first week or so, I would wander the paddocks with them as they adjusted to life with Archie and me. They would roam the paddocks, always trotting up at dinner time. My paddocks were green and had a lot of grass for the two of them. Chant was an old horse at the ripe age of 29. She had been one of the first horses I had ridden and was a great beginners/novice horse. She loved being a kids' lesson horse and was so gentle and smooth to ride.

Minty was 18 years old and had been my instructor's husband's horse. I hadn't ridden her before. She was a little taller than Chant and loved trail-riding. She was a little more advanced in her movements and my instructor was hoping we would make a good team.

After the horses arrived at my place, my instructor started to come to me for my lessons, which were now an hour. I had a couple of areas that were flat that we could work on, and I mostly rode Minty to build my skills and relationship with her. I continued to ride Chant when we were starting to canter as she had a smoother stride than Minty.

After having them with me for a few weeks, my confidence started to drop. I would get on Chant and try to move her, but she was so stubborn that she didn't want to budge. I would get off her, walk her around and try again, but to no avail as she just didn't want me to ride her.

I decided to try to ride Minty. She was being a little stubborn, but not as bad as Chant. Then, as we were walking, she would stop raise her left hind leg and kick my ankle. She would continue to do this a few more times, until I started to get a bit scared. Fear rose in me that she might buck me off and I would get injured. Because I was on my property by myself, if I had a bad fall, it would take some time to get someone to come and help me.

That day, the fear overrode my desire to ride. I had to get off in tears. I went up to both horses, asking them why they didn't want me to ride them and why they had made me so scared that fear overtook my passion. Of course, they didn't answer; rather, they walked off into the paddock to graze, happy not to have me on their backs.

I was devastated. I started to overthink whether I had done the right thing by leasing them. Maybe they didn't fit with me or me with them, and this was all just a little too much for me. I ruminated on this for days, that my dream of owning a horse may not become a reality, and I was so upset.

After a few days, I decided to book a lesson with my instructor after telling her what had gone on. Of course, when she got on both, they acted like perfect horses. But what she did tell me is that we had a tug of war of who was boss. They both wanted to show me they were the boss, and of course I was letting this happen because I feared the consequences.

I rode both that day and exerted extra confidence. My instructor gave me some additional tips to use when they tried it on me next time, basically turning them in circles when they didn't do what I was asking them. Horses don't like doing this as it makes them uncomfortable, so this is a far better approach than using force.

After a few more attempts on my own with each of them, they started to work with me. I am not the perfect rider and am always learning, but I have worked out that when I have given my girls a confusing command, this is usually when they react to me. I now always apologise and rub their necks saying, 'That was my fault, let's try it again.' I persist until we have succeeded, and as soon as we have, my lesson is done.

Over the next three months leading up to Christmas, and not being able to travel interstate due to Covid, I really started to build a great relationship with both of them. I found that the more groundwork I did, working them on a long lead rope rather than riding them every time, the less tension there was between the three of us.

Chant, my old girl, wouldn't walk on the lead rope so I would sometimes have to use the crop and tap her on the rump for her to walk. She was starting to walk with me more times than not which was progress. Minty wasn't doing as many cow kicks, and I was loving getting her into a trot and practicing the rising trot position.

What I found most profound over this period was that as I started to calm down, so did they. Every day that I would go to feed them, I would stand beside them and rub their necks as they were eating. Chant didn't like it at first and would walk away from her hay so that I wouldn't pat her while she was eating. But after a few months, she started to ease into the routine and stay there to enjoy the love I was giving her.

Chant would also do what I would call a 'chomp'. When I did something to her – grooming, feeding, putting her saddle on – she would turn her head towards me and go to bite me. She never connected, but it was a warning to say, 'I don't like this, stop it.' I watched some videos on this and they said the worst thing you can do is step away from her after she's done it.

The more I worked with her, the more confidence I developed. Knowing she probably wasn't going to connect, I started to step into her after she did this and would rub her cheeks. After a few months, the chomps became less frequent, and she would stand and let me do most things without getting annoyed.

The relationship I was building, one of mutual respect and love between these animals and myself, was having a profound effect on me. Like with Archie, if I was sad, I would go into the paddock and just sit with the horses. I always knew not to ride them when I was in a tough place because my feelings would be felt through them and they may react in an adverse manner.

I would stroke their necks whilst feeding them, watch them walking in the paddock, and mow or weed the paddock while they were standing near me. These all allowed me to feel a sense of calmness, and even healing, that I needed after the combined trauma of the previous 18 months.

They were becoming my soulmates, like my boy Archie – teaching me without judgment or criticism how to be in the moment. When I am out riding my girls, all I think about is being in the moment and giving them so much love and care.

In return, they give me love, respect and purpose. Purpose in that they depend on me to be fed, cared for and loved. That I am a trusted human who will always look after them. That I won't hurt them and I will respect their emotions, especially on off days when they don't want me to ride them.

When I am trotting or cantering through my paddocks, my horses give me the freedom and feeling that I am alive. They fill my heart, make me smile and give me the confidence that I deserve to be their owner, their mum, the one that they can depend on.

In January 2021, I approached my riding instructor and asked if she would sell the girls to me. After five months of having them at my property, I had built this love with these animals that I didn't want to let go. They had taught me so much and had been so patient with me, and they were now part of my family.

Thankfully, she said yes. She couldn't think of a better place for them both to grow old. They were both in amazing conditions, she could see that I looked after them and she loved that they had these beautiful green pastures to graze on.

I was over the moon. I had made my childhood dream a reality and I could have these two with me until the end of their days.

Once I bought them, I felt my confidence around them increase. All our faults started to lessen. I felt that my riding was improving even more, and they were becoming very well-adjusted to me.

In February 2021, I started to take Minty on trail rides with my neighbour, Romy, and her horse, Lily. At first, Chant was really upset that I had left her in the paddock by herself and she wasn't coming. When my god-daughter Abby came up to stay in March, all three of us went out riding. Abby on Minty and I rode Chant. Chant loved taking the lead coming out on the road with us. Abby having grown up taking lessons herself, couldn't get enough rides in during her time up visiting me.

The 10 days that her sister, Caitlin, came up in February and Abby in March with their boyfriends were an amazing time with the horses. All four of them rode the girls. Abby took the lead with her boyfriend, who hadn't ridden before. Caitlin and her boyfriend were a little more tentative but still loved being able to ride and feel more confident on a horse.

I loved being able to take everything that my instructor had taught me and pass it on to them. It felt a little weird, instructing them after I had only learnt myself from an expert over the last year. I wanted them to learn like I learnt, but more than anything, to enjoy the feeling of being one with a horse and feeling the adrenaline and beauty of these amazing animals. It was something I wanted to share.

After they had all gone back to Melbourne, I continued to ride with Romy once or twice a week depending on our schedules. I love going out with her. She has ridden horses nearly all her life and has a very good horse mind. We also get to catch up, chat and have lots of laughs. She gives me confidence riding with her, and I know my riding has continued to improve as a result.

Since riding with Romy and having to leave Chant in the paddock by herself, I started to yearn for a third horse.

I wanted a third horse for a few reasons. Firstly, to always have two horses in the paddock, to comfort each other when I rode with Romy. Secondly, having horses that are aged 29 and 18, they won't live forever, so I thought getting a younger horse will always ensure I have two together to keep each other company. Thirdly, I wanted to continue to improve my skills on a bigger and more challenging horse.

At the start of May 2021, I saw a post by my instructor that she had to sell another horse. Her name was Piper, an 11-year-old thoroughbred, 15.2hh, 6 foot. She needed someone to work her, as she hadn't been able to do much with her as she had four other horses herself.

I immediately messaged her saying I was interested and asked her if she thought I could learn to ride her. I also wanted to make sure my two would be able to adjust to a third horse and they could all live in harmony.

My instructor was rapt that I answered the call. She said she and her husband couldn't think of a better place for her to live out her days. I went over to meet Piper. I had seen her being ridden by stronger riders in the past year, and as soon as I saw her again, I was in love. I don't even know why I had to see her to say yes. My mind was already made up about buying her and I just knew she had to come home with me.

The following week, two horses became three – three beauties that would bring me even more love, calm, peace and serenity. The first few days of having Piper were a bit of a challenge, especially for Chant. She had been the alpha, but now Piper was here to take over. Although Piper is now the alpha, she and Chant have a respect for each other in the paddock most days and Minty and Piper have such a beautiful relationship.

Piper was always going to be a challenge, which I knew from the day I enquired about her. She was at a different level than I had ridden before. She had had an injury that meant I couldn't ride her immediately and she was a lot bigger than my other two horses.

For the first four months, I did a lot of groundwork with her – meaning not riding her, and instead putting her in a halter and walking her around, first on flat ground, then around obstacles so we could build our relationship. She was a little feisty at first and was very unsettled with the farrier. I had to be calm when around her as I could tell she was picking up on my uneasiness.

I was determined that we would form a great relationship, so over those months I read lots of books from reputable horse experts, watched countless videos and listened to podcasts. I wanted to equip myself with the best techniques and start to foster a strong bond with my horses.

As the weeks went by, the time I spent with Piper became more frequent and I could see that she trusted me more every week. Horses are so in tune with your body language, behaviour and feelings. I was starting to appreciate and understand the way Piper was in tune with everything I was feeling and we started to build mutual respect.

More than anything, I loved this horse. A few people had told me to be careful, that she is an ex-racehorse, she has had trauma and I needed to keep my safety in mind as the priority. As I started to work her in my new round yard, she became calmer and more attentive. She knew that when we walked in there, it was time to work. I got her to a stage where she would start walking beside me without a halter and I had started to ease my weight on her back in readiness to put a saddle on.

I had learnt all these techniques from the best and it was starting to build my confidence, ease my doubts and enable me to enjoy being around this beautiful horse. She had a charm that I couldn't resist, and when I saw her canter or gallop up the paddock, I couldn't wait to ride her and enjoy the love we were building.

I can't get enough of learning from Warwick Schiller and several other horse people. The approach they take is building the relationship on the ground. A horse doesn't need to be ridden five times a week, and I wanted to get the relationship right before anything else.

I also watched a movie called *Buck,* the true story of a horseman called Buck Brannaman. His techniques are exactly what I believe in: don't reprimand, be kind and always reward good responses by your horse. What he does is train the human, not the horse. The human needs to have the right disposition before the horse will.

I am totally focusing on this and getting so much joy from it to the point where after I watched the video, I took Archie and we sat in the paddock watching the horses. I thought of nothing else but observing my horses and then my eyes started to well up with tears. I started to get all warm inside and a few tears slid down my cheeks. They were tears of joy of what an amazing life I have with my three girls and Archie. I am learning to become a new version of myself: kinder, more loving and more giving, and my horses are responding so magically as a result.

It didn't take long before I had built up the confidence to ride Piper. I ride her once a week and do groundwork two to three times a week. She is very smart, and I am getting better with my commands and not confusing her. We have progressed to a trot and doing figure eights and four rings in the round yard. I have cantered her once and to say I need a lot more work on her is an understatement. But I know we will get there, and we have come so far already.

In the two years since starting riding lessons, leasing Charmaine and then buying my three girls, I now understand how powerful horses are when it comes to healing. I can see why they are so amazing with people who suffer from disabilities and PTSD. Their nature that can calm the soul and lift the spirit is so evident once you spend lots of time with them.

In October, I decided to undertake an introductory equine therapy course. I believe that there are some simple methods that I can develop to help people to reduce their fear of horses, and fear in general. I really hope that the sessions that I develop will be part of my future retreats once the cabins are built. I can't wait to share my horses with my guests and enable them to feel their love and to bring them joy.

My horses continue to teach me calmness, peace, patience, respect and trust. They never ask anything of me and have helped heal my heart from the pain of losing my husband. Robert had the foresight to tell me that I could buy a horse when we first moved here, and I have fulfilled my dream and his wishes.

When I am with my horses, Robert is always in my heart. I ride my girls with such respect and compassion. I love the feeling, the freedom and the unconditional love and care you get from these beautiful animals.

My Lesson for You:

- Animals have the biggest hearts and will teach you more than any human will.
- My compassion, patience, calmness, fear and love has changed as a result of them.
- Animals live in the moment and are never thinking about the past or future. We need to be more like them, to live our lives in the now.
- Sit and watch animals, whether they are your own, someone else's or at a zoo. We can learn a lot from observing them.
- If you get the opportunity to be around a horse, take the time to pat them, watch them and see how they react to you. If you take deep breaths and reduce your heart rate, I am sure they will be more at ease with you.

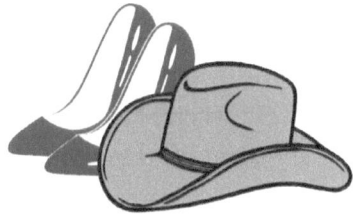

Chapter 11

Getting Down and Dirty

Before Robert died, we had discussed the projects that we wanted to complete on our property. Thankfully, the house and sheds didn't need anything done to them, but we wanted to add extra areas to enjoy the amazing views year-round.

The first tasks were completed by my brother Paul and Robert's mates, James and Shane. Early in 2019, when Robert was in hospital, the three guys decided to come up from Melbourne and do a few projects for us. Our pool had been put in and we needed some new fences to keep our dogs contained.

The trip, when it eventuated, was also when Robert was in palliative care and dying. The boys had not only arrived to do the work they had planned to do, now with my dad, but also to say their goodbyes to Robert. Having to come up and say their goodbyes, made them more determined to get the jobs done.

Over four days, they built two fences and a retaining wall path. They worked their guts out and finished the project on the day Robert died. A day of mixed emotions, but when I came home after leaving Robert for the last time, I was so proud of what the guys had achieved.

On the night that Robert died, we decided to burn the bamboo that he had cut down earlier in the year in his memory. Robert hated that bamboo, so it was perfect to sit around it, reminiscing about the memories we had shared with him and watch the bamboo burn to the ground. Having the boys up here was emotional, but so beautiful. They had done an amazing job for a man they loved and treasured.

I am very lucky to have two great mates in Queensland, John and Steve, who love using their hands and building stuff. I had a shed of amazing tools that could do most jobs and over the years Robert and I were married, almost every Christmas I would buy Robert a power tool. There was always a tool that he wanted to be able to complete projects around the house whether in Melbourne or Brisbane.

When we bought Coolabine, there were several additional tools/toys that we needed, and we were starting to create a great tool shed to be able to tackle several projects ourselves.

The first major project in 2020 was the fire pit that sits in front of the patio. Steve was available to come up for four days and him and I built it together. I had ordered the sleepers that would frame the area up, but firstly, we had to dig out the site. I worked out it was a lot easier to build projects the size the wood is already cut to, so the area ended up being 4.8 metres by 2.4 metres.

Let the digging begin. It took us a full day to dig the site down to the required level. All of it was done with a crowbar, shovel and mattock. Hours of digging, coming across rocks and then pipes. Pipes that I didn't know what they were, so we had to be very careful to ensure we only cut out the pipes we didn't need with the help of my neighbour, the previous owner.

The second day kicked off with a trip to Bunnings and Iron Bark Timbers to get the wood for the seats that would sit in front of the retaining walls. We picked up the pine from Bunnings, then went to Iron Bark and on the way out, an employee asked us if we were building an outside structure, and we replied that we were. He told us that the wood we had bought was internal pine and within two years it would rot with the weather. He said we needed to buy H3 pine which is treated for outdoor use.

Both Steve and I looked at either and said, 'F**k.' Back to Bunnings we went. We sat in the line-up with all the other tradespeople who obviously knew what they were doing, and we swapped over the wood. Our two-hour trip to the coast to pick up the supplies had now increased to three hours and to say we were frustrated by our amateur mistake is an understatement!

The afternoon of day two was all about finalising the building of the retaining walls. We got to work and didn't finish building until 6 pm. Our bodies ached after the last two days. I hadn't done this type of manual work before. We were working with plans Steve had written up. They weren't the best drawings, but we were winging parts of it and doing a great job!

Steve and I, and even Robert when he was alive, worked well together. I am always happy to do the hard work. At one stage we needed a couple of holes dug for the retaining wall posts and the dirt was so hard. With my trusty garden spade – yes, a small hand spade that you usually use in a garden bed – I knelt on my knees and dug a 500mm-deep hole. It took me over an hour, but when you don't have a post hole digger or a jack hammer, which Steve wanted to hire, you just get holes dug with whatever you have.

Along the way, we had a few laughs. I think at some points Steve wanted to kill me by not spending the money to hire the equipment, but this was a monumental build. The first I had done with a mate, the first that Robert had wanted and the first that would be in remembrance of Robert. There was deep emotion involved. I think for us to get back up on day three and four, we called out to Robert to help us on many occasions!

Day three started with laying the road base which was the floor of the fire pit. Of course, barrowing the road base in wasn't an easy task. I have a paved rocky path into the front of the house with a small gate. We basically had to do a run-up with each barrow on boards to get it in. While I barrowed and tipped the road base into the area, Steve shovelled and spread the base.

After an hour, we got the barrowing done, flattened it with a roller and watered it in.

Next up was building the seats. The retaining wall had already been built by my brother and Robert's mates a year ago so erecting that seating area was a reasonably easy task. We attached the seat on the back of the retaining area which saved both money and time.

We decided that we would build the other two seats in the shed. They wouldn't attach to the side retaining walls as I wanted to be able to move them closer to the fire pit depending on how many people and how cold it was when we sat around it. Together we worked on building the first seat. Measuring once, measuring twice. Leveling once, leveling twice. At times we didn't get every measurement right and had to recut, but generally our ability to work together was damn good.

We finished the first chair, which was two metres by 700mm and around 500mm high. It was made of H3 pine covered with recycled wood panelling. It was now time to move it into the fire pit area which was about 70 metres from the sheds, and you needed to drop down into the lawn area to place it into the pit area.

One, two, three, lift… OMG! Neither of us realised how heavy these seats were going to be. They were double my expectation, and thankfully, I have some level of strength as they were heavy. After a few more expletives, we carried the chair into the patio area, down into the lawn and sat it in place. I think at this point Steve and I were about to have heart attacks.

It had taken all our strength and Robert's help from above to move these from the shed. But once it was in place and we levelled it on the road base, it looked amazing. It was at this point we discussed whether they would ever be moved. Maybe not – we would see how we go with the next chair. But that was tomorrow's challenge. It was getting dark and time to retire for the night.

Over these three nights, we weren't having any late ones or drinking much. We were exhausted every night. On the third night, with the new fire pit that I had also purchased from Bunnings, it was time to light her up. What a sight! Steve and I, with a glass of red wine in hand, said cheers to ourselves and to Robert. What an amazing task so far and the reward of sitting in front of that fire, eating dinner and drinking red wine had been all worth it.

Our last day was much of the same as the previous day. We made a couple of measuring errors on the last seat. Probably because we had been going for three days. Steve was leaving that day and I was pushing to get it finished and finish we did. Again, we had the joy of moving the seat into place. After four days of moving sleepers, digging the pit out, building the chairs our muscles weren't as strong as they had been. We got it into place, but Jesus, it hurt to do so!

As we stood back and looked at what we had built, we were damn proud of ourselves. With little experience and a plan that a child could have drawn, we had built a fire pit together. I couldn't have been happier and I knew Robert would have been smiling from above, damn proud of us too. It was unconventional building at times, but we had done it, our way! I couldn't thank Steve enough for his time, skills and mateship!

A couple of months later, on the first anniversary of Robert's death, I had friends over to celebrate Robert's life. As part of that, we lit the fire pit. Steve surprised me with a plaque he had made up that would sit on the wall of the fire pit in memory of Robert. We dedicated the new sign and pit to Robert's life. It was such a beautiful gesture, and that plaque sits proudly for all to see.

GETTING DOWN AND DIRTY

Steve came back a few weeks later after we built the fire pit. It was the coldest weekend that we had in 2020 only getting to eight degrees on the Saturday, our main building day! But that wasn't going to stop us from getting a few small projects done. We finished the fire pit area by building a path down to it. We built a gate at the end of the pool to keep the front area secure and a new fence between the pool and garden again to secure the area where Archie played and slept.

This time, digging the holes was a lot easier. Steve's dad, Daryll, had gifted his electric jack hammer to me. He had sent it up to Steve's and because he didn't need it anymore – his jack hammering days were over and Steve lived in a townhouse – he wanted me to have it. Such a beautiful gesture that made a world of difference.

Over the course of two days, we completed the small projects and enhanced our building skills. After erecting the fence that week, I painted it and it made such a difference to the front of the house.

Now I didn't have to worry about Archie getting out or wild dogs or foxes getting in. Another task had been completed and I was so proud of our work.

The third project was a deck in front of the sheds behind the house. Over the previous nine months, I had worked with several friends to clear the bushes that hid the view to the west. It was an amazing view that captured the rolling mountains of Conondale National Park.

Now it was time to build the deck. John and Steve were both up to help me. We started it the day after Robert's one-year anniversary. Waking up that day, we were a little under the weather, and I especially felt for Steve who, as always, loves a drink, especially in memory of his mate.

The day after Robert's memorial dinner, the boys started building the deck, and, of course, the holes had to be dug first – all twelve of them that would hold the structure. Steve on the jackhammer had the job of digging. With sweat rolling down his face, he dug hole after hole. A lot of water and Gatorade were drunk that day. They did a great job under the circumstances.

That afternoon, Steve got a call from work. He is a mine manager in Papua New Guinea and was required to go back to work in two days. This meant Steve had to get on the road that afternoon and the building, painting of the deck boards was now a job for John, Di and I.

Over the next two days, we painted, built the structure and secured the decking boards. I don't know how many damn screws I inserted into that deck, but we could have a cyclone come through Coolabine and that deck won't go anywhere.

John taught me lots of different building terms and different ways to get things done, including that measuring and leveling were two of the most important parts of the job. I also learnt about joists, bearers and beams and how to use an impact drill. The end product looks sensational, and I regularly enjoy many sunsets out there with Archie, family or friends. It is a frequent talking point and is the perfect place to relax after a long day.

The last project John, Di and I completed in preparation for the cabins to be built was a new chicken coop and two retaining walls behind the sheds. The driveway between my tanks would allow access to the cabin site when building started, so it needed to be built before the cabin plans went to the council for approval.

The chicken coop was the first project on the list, then it was back to digging again. But this time I had borrowed my neighbours post hole digger. In total, we dug 17 holes between the two projects, each one at least 600mm deep. We struck varying soil types over the first 11 holes of the chicken coop. Sand, clay, rocks and dirt in all colours.

Some holes were dug in 20 minutes, but the majority took 30 minutes with a couple taking longer and that was with a post hole digger.

By the end of day one, we had nearly all the holes dug, a few poles in and were on our way. Over the next few days, it was erecting poles, cementing them in and building the structure. John is a particularly good builder. Everything is centimetre perfect which at times, irritated me because it was just a chook shed, but as John reminded me, if I wanted his help, I needed to build it like this. I didn't know what I was doing, I was learning, so I needed all his help and I needed to be patient.

Di and I went to the salvage and bought used Colourbond panels that would form the bottom of the coop, the back walls and roof. That was an experience and the guys there were so accommodating, and we got a good deal. Plus, this was all part of the adventure and I do like reusing materials rather than always buying new stuff.

After John cut the sheeting and taught me how to use a grinder safely, we put the panels in place and it was all starting to come together. The following day, we placed the chicken wire over the roof and walls and we had a new chook coop. It had taken five days to erect and looked amazing. My five girls even had a view out to the Conondale mountains. Lucky chickens!

After moving the chickens, we then needed to take down the old chicken coop. We engaged the assistance of my neighbour with his tractor to do the hard stuff. John, Di and I had taken down the walls, roofing, wire and poles that we could. However, my neighbour who built this structure had done an awesome job concerting some of the poles in and we couldn't move them.

Then came more digging. This time it was for the retaining walls to form the driveway out to the ridge for the cabins. Now these were hard. Thankfully, we had two extra pairs of hands for the day. Mitch and Kyran came up for the afternoon and night and Mitch helped us dig the remaining holes. But we ran into trouble. Whilst digging the second last hole, we broke the post hole digger. The rock had been harder than we expected, and the top of the digger broke off the engine area.

From here, it was back to the jack hammer and crowbar. At times, we even got the jack hammer stuck in between rocks. It seemed to take hours to dig one hole and we were exhausted. The next day John and I dug the last hole, mostly by the crowbar and shovel. It took us over an hour, and we were bloody happy when it was done. We then built the walls with sleepers, following John's lead. After a load of road base/crushed rock was delivered and spread, my retaining walls and structures were complete.

We completed two major projects over the 10-day period. I couldn't thank John and Di enough. When Di wasn't helping us, she had been making us breakfast, lunch and dinner. Cold drinks and tea in between and Kyran and her had even washed my windows for me. What amazing friends I had! I couldn't thank them enough.

GETTING DOWN AND DIRTY

These two projects were essential preparation for the cabins. I needed them built in advance so that trucks and labourers had a clear path through to the building site. On the last night, we rewarded ourselves with a good bottle of bubbles on the deck. Our cheers were to a job well done, friendship and future success.

Those holes had tested my patience, resilience and strength. When you are so determined to complete a project, that's what gets you through. John and I had been on the tools for the last week and we certainly weren't as energised as we were on day one. Plus, you are working with a mate, and I don't know how things work in the trade, so I had to be guided by John, which was new for me. When I worked in my corporate role, I was the leader, so I wasn't used to be being the apprentice.

I had totally changed my role in this world. From leading people and teams. Working with contractors, executives. Going into the office or meeting people in the field and making decisions on strategy and how we operated our teams. Now I was down in the dirt literally. Digging holes, pouring cement, drilling and screwing structures together and being on my feet all day – a total change from a year ago.

But the one thing I knew from this tree change was the satisfaction of building something yourself. Starting with nothing and then standing back in awe and with pride in the job you did yourself with your mates. I may have broken every nail on my hands, had dirt in my ears every day and dragged my body into bed thinking I couldn't do it all again tomorrow, but I had done it for 10 days straight with John and Di and we had accomplished great things.

All these projects were completed in the first year without Robert with two dear friends. They were two of Robert's best mates and he would never have let them down, nor they him. I know that while each project was being completed, they would've thought of Robert, maybe even talked to Robert. They probably told him that they will always have my back, they will always be there for me, and they wanted to play a part in me fulfilling my dream.

The projects didn't stop there though. I was determined to do as many as I could myself before work on the cabins started. I decided to install two new water tanks next to the house as I wanted to make sure I had enough water for myself and the cabins before they opened. The first tank went in in January 2020 and my neighbour John, Steve and his dad, Daryll, helped me to put it in place. The tanks were large at 22,500 litres each.

The second tank was put in six months later. When the second arrived, they brought it up on the truck right next to the house. With John my neighbour's help, we decided we could tip the tank off the truck close to the house and then push it along the concrete another 10 metres and it would be in place.

The whole time the delivery guy was there, he kept referring to John on where to put it and how to do it. Just because John had organised the first tank for me, and he had had a few delivered himself, didn't mean I should be shut out. This was my house, but this guy was not even talking to me. I continued to take his instructions and we tipped the tank onto the concrete.

By then, I was getting pretty fed up with him not taking my instructions, so when he asked the next question, I spoke over John saying, 'Yes, I would like the tank moved to there as it's my house.' But the guy kept talking to John, and although I was the one instructing him, I thought he never really respected me. I took the paperwork and said thanks for installing it at my house. He didn't even flinch, and then off he went.

It is frustrating when you aren't respected for the work that you do, even if it is just helping someone to do it. There are just some men in the world that still believe this is a man's world, and I think they are uncomfortable working with women.

Over the next 12 months, I continued to clear areas in the paddocks, spraying weeds in the paddock and planting new trees. At the top of the driveway, I planted an area with my friend Claire, that is now full of grevilleas. The grevilleas once grown, will be a haven for the birds when the flowers bloom. I also started the task of planting trees down my driveway. They will take a while to grow, and the driveway is 330 metres long, but I have started and everything is growing well to date.

In June 2021, I asked my neighbour John to build three horse yards for me. Now with three horses, having these yards would allow me to feed them without them pinching each other's food. It would be a lot easier for me to manage when the farrier or vet had to come out and it was a lot safer for me. I had already been caught up in a battle of the mares over food without the yards and I was worried I may fall victim to their strength.

Over four days, my neighbour was the leader and I was the apprentice. We dug 12 holes and this time he bought the big toy in, a post hole digger that was on the front of his tractor. Now digging holes was a much quicker process with his machinery. I would judge whether the holes were being dug in the right position and take out any dirt that went back into the holes after removal.

We then put the poles in, backfilled the dirt and attached the bottom rail – measuring, cutting and leveling before drilling them into the poles. Then came the top rail, which was attached by a method called a cobb and co hitch. It is what the farmers use to build fences before any fancy bolts and drills were introduced.

My neighbour showed me how to drill two holes in each pole, then thread through a piece of wire that is doubled over for strength, before winding the wire. It was such great practice and it came up so well. Lastly, we attached the chains at the back of the entrance to all three horse yards.

At one point when we were building, my neighbour said, 'Listen to the sounds.' I stopped talking and just listened. He said, 'Listen to nothing.' You could have heard a pin drop. There was no machinery, no cars, no wind, nothing at all. This moment in time gave me goosebumps. I appreciated the stillness a rural environment gives you. These are the times that I am grateful for where I live!

In July 2021, my Queensland parents, Ally and Daryll, came to stay with me for 10 days. I was supposed to go to Melbourne, but due to Covid in Queensland, I couldn't get approval from the Victorian Government to visit, so I stayed at home and Ally and Daryll came up to visit instead.

For the first five days, we painted the fence behind the house. The fence had been there since we bought the house and after I had installed two new tanks behind it, I wanted to paint the fence black, which matched the guttering, windows on the house and cleaned up the area. I am a bit of a stickler for having things looking neat and tidy. I am sure Robert looks down from above shaking his head saying, 'Yes, dear, that is your OCD in overdrive!'

We started painting with brushes on the first day and then Daryll suggested we buy a spray gun as it would cut down the time and effort and have a much more consistent finish. Off to Bunnings we went with a list of additional items that we needed, for other repairs that week.

What a godsend that spray gun was. It took us a little bit to get the right paint consistency to cover the fence, but once that was done and Daryll built a frame for the sheeting that went behind the fence so the trees and house didn't get painted.

Three days later, by the time we had put two coats on the fence, the job was done. It looks amazing; I had a new toy in the tool shed and every day I look at my newly painted fence, I smile with pride.

The next project was a new veggie patch. When John and Di helped me to build and knock down the old chook shed, I had let the space behind the sheds, turn into an out-of-control vegie patch. The seeds from the pumpkins, capsicums and tomatoes that had been left in the soil from the chooks over the last year had now blossomed and was starting to spread everywhere.

Over the last few weeks before Daryll had come up, I had removed most of the veggies, which was after harvesting over 25 pumpkins and hundreds of tomatoes. I had turned the tomatoes into relish and passata and had an area that I wanted to fence off and replant.

The patch was around 5.5 metres squared and would be supported by five round pine poles, with star pickets in between them and wrapped with chicken wire. The digging of the holes was relatively easy. Easy compared to some of the other holes that have been dug in the paddocks. We didn't hit much rock and it was only the clay that made the digging a little harder.

With our trusty measuring tape, level and quick-set concrete, we had the poles in on the first day, ready to set over night. The next day we put the star pickets in and started to put the holding wire between the poles. This was to make sure the chicken wire stayed in place and didn't sag.

The wrapping of the chicken wire took some time. By the time we measured the wire, cut it, hung it and started to attach it to the draw lines, it was a team effort by both of us.

During the hanging process, I was introduced to a new tool: a wire joiner. This tool has wire rings that you clamp together to hang the wire. I am only just a little competitive and bringing out my corporate KPIs gave Daryll and I a quality target of who could clamp these small wires without dropping them.

The competition was on. Daryll started first but, unfortunately, he hadn't mastered his technique and so he fell short of the 95 per cent target. Then it was my turn… and off I went! Never one to miss a target, I achieved 100 per cent. I was given the task to do the rest of the clamping because I was so good at it. We created some fun out of a mundane task and had quite a few laughs while doing it.

Over two days, we had built the veggie patch and being the perfectionist that Daryll is, he wasn't totally satisfied with the tension in the wire, so tightened it all up. After I installed the chain to secure the gate, the task was complete. Now, it was back to me to fill and turn over the dirt with horse manure and start planting my veggies.

I am hoping that once the cabins are open, I will be self-sufficient when it comes to providing veggies for my guests and allows me to teach their children how to create their own veggie patches at home, whether in the backyard or in pots.

I love learning new skills and having the right skilled people teaching me what to do. I would never attempt a project without these guys and the time we are together doing it is priceless. My neighbour always has some interesting facts and knowledge to tell me when he is helping me with a project. We have a great working relationship and after doing something a few times, I start to get into a rhythm of what he needs in what sequence, and he seems happy working with me.

What a new world I was a part of! These were big achievements which gave me the greatest rewards and I couldn't be prouder of what I was building. I will never go back to the corporate wardrobe again. Jeans, work shirts, steel-cap boots and caps are my new uniform – and I love it!

My Lesson for You:

- Give things a try. You will never know when you may need that skill or knowledge in the future.
- Don't be scared of hard work. Hard work reaps rewards.
- The feeling of satisfaction of a job well done is what gives you the confidence to do it again.
- If you need help, ask someone. All of these projects have been a team effort. People love helping others, so let them help you.
- Starting something new can be scary especially if you haven't done it before. Consult the experts and do it properly the first time.

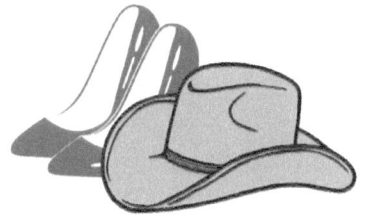

Chapter 12

Creatures Great and Small

One part of living in the country is that there are a lot of creatures that cross your path. Before I moved to Coolabine, I had only seen a couple of snakes. I screamed every time I saw them, or, if in the car, I would jump up in my seat to get away from them. Not sure that was necessary, but that's how fearful I was of them.

I knew one day I would have to come face-to-face with reptiles. I would also have to get used to foxes and wild dogs being on the property as we lived on the back of a national park. There would also be birds flying about, which if they came near my head, I would always scream. Just ask my goddaughters and bestie – they think it's hilarious when birds swoop on me!

For the first year of living at Coolabine, I only saw snakes on the road. The nearest to the house was at the front gate which is around 450 metres away. It was a red belly black snake and as soon as it felt the vibrations from the car it slithered off into the paddock.

I also saw another red belly on my driveway, as well as a green tree snake. Again, both looked up and then slithered quickly into the paddocks. On both occasions, I slowed down to see where it was off to. I didn't want to run over them. I was becoming quite inquisitive and was kind of excited to finally see them.

Mum and Dad saw the first one when I was in Brisbane in 2019, caring for Robert while he was in hospital. They were minding the house and went into the chook shed one day when Mum saw this big python. She jumped back and I am sure she let a few swear words drop. She showed Dad and because he was a metre or so behind the laying boxes and the eggs, she quickly got the eggs and ran out.

The coastal python stayed in the chook shed for a few days. It seemed he had eaten a rat and was taking protection in the chook shed digesting his meal. He moved a little bit but not too much. Mum got used to going in there to collect the eggs without being too frightened. Because she liked his colours, she decided to call him Pete.

Pete has visited the chook shed several times, the last time being in October 2021. He is such a good-looking snake and has never eaten a chicken or egg. He goes into the chook shed to hide and digest and then is gone within a few days. I have gotten used to him and the only time I have ever seen him outside of the chook shed is when he was in my second shed on top of the hot water system. My neighbour who used to own the property said he has been there for years, but he had seen him a few times in the shed during winter hibernating.

The first snake I came across in the paddock was when I was taking Archie for a walk in December 2020. Because Archie was at the stage of chasing cows, I had him on a long lead that day.

We were walking back to the driveway when he bolted on me and I nearly fell over. About 10 metres away I could see a red belly that seemed to be twisting. I quickly pulled Archie back so that he didn't get bitten and took a few steps forward. It seemed unusual for a snake not to move off when it felt vibrations, but this one wasn't moving.

I got my camera out and zoomed in to take a photo. Archie was next to me, itching to run over there and see what was happening. Still, the snake wasn't moving. I decided we needed to move on in case we had outstayed our welcome.

When I relooked at the photos later, I noticed that there were two snakes wrapped around each other, possibly mating. It was September, which is breeding season, and thankfully they were literally too wrapped up in what they were doing to notice Archie and I.

Seeing these two snakes in the paddock, although it got my heartbeat racing, I was happy that I had stood still and just watched. They say you shouldn't run away from snakes, although I wouldn't have thought I could stand still watching them even two years ago. Maybe I can appreciate these reptiles and we can both live in harmony at Coolabine Retreat.

I saw my first snake up at the house in November 2020. I was sitting on the patio and could hear a green frog croaking, but it sounded different. It was coming from behind the house, so I went to investigate. There it was, a small snake, moving outside my laundry door. The area is concrete and it kept ducking behind the old dog kennel.

I couldn't really get a good glimpse of it and didn't know what it was. It seemed to be dark, and I sent a few photos to some friends that said it might be a brown snake.

If it was a brown snake, I needed to get it removed as I didn't want it to go around the front of the house where Archie was. I rang a snake catcher who arrived an hour later. While I was waiting, I just sat in the laundry, watching where it was as I didn't want to lose sight of it.

After moving the dog kennel, they caught the snake. It was a non-venomous green tree snake. I felt a bit silly having rung them, but it was the first time a snake had come to the house and I wasn't aware of the different types. They removed the snake and took it away. They probably let it go down the road, seeing that the area is all rural properties!

Just before Christmas in 2020, another green snake visited the house. This time I knew from the colourings it was a green tree snake and it was non-venomous. I decided I wasn't going to pay $100 to have it removed. It could get very expensive for me if I had to have a snake removed every month.

I was mesmerised by this green snake with a striking blue and yellow belly. It would sit up, with its big eyes, doing a little dance, moving side to side. The frogs that were under the gas bottles attached to the back of the house had attracted it. Green tree snakes feast on frogs. I don't know if it ate any, but I loved observing this snake from the safety of the laundry door. After a few hours it disappeared, probably after getting its meal.

After Christmas, the green snake returned one more time, this time at the end of the house to feast on green frogs under my water tank. Again, I heard the croaking, and knew what it was. I quietly stepped around the tanks with my gumboots on and there it was with its tail halfway out from under the tanks.

This time, my parents and my goddaughter Caitlin, were there. I told them what it was and that if they wanted to see it, to come quickly around the tanks. Everybody exclaimed, 'Wow, it's so close! It's not moving.' Caitlin took some photos, and for an 18-year-old city girl, I was very proud of her calmness.

It didn't disturb us, and it didn't come into the front patio area. So, we left it there, to try and get a meal. I decided that because he had visited a couple of times, he needed to have a name, so I called him George and I hope he comes back to visit next summer.

In 2021, being less fearful of snakes, I started to see a lot more. My first encounter with an eastern brown snake was about 50 metres from the top of my driveway.

Mum and Dad had arrived at my place in January. I had wanted to take my ride on mower down to the bottom of the driveway to mow the horse paddock. I hadn't done it before because I was worried it wasn't stable enough and it might tip over. Anytime I want to try something new, I always have people around to do it with, just in case something goes wrong.

With my parents at the top of the driveway, I headed down. As I got 50 metres from the top, I saw an eastern brown in the drain on the left-hand side of the driveway, probably 10 metres away. I stopped the ride-on and just let it idle as I watched watch the 1.5-metre snake slither across the driveway to the right-hand side and into the paddock.

Once I saw its tail disappear, I turned the ride-on around and headed back up to my parents. When I came back so quickly, they thought it had been unsafe to take the ride-on down. I said, 'No, let's go closer to the house and I will show you what I saw.' I had been able to get my phone out and video the snake moving across the driveway.

They said, 'Wow, where did it go?' 'Into the paddock, I think,' I replied. 'I think it's better that you go up to the house. I'll continue down the driveway and you'll be able to see me from the top. I'll wait a couple of minutes before heading down to make sure it's fully disappeared.'

Other than seeing a brown snake in the Northern Territory (that story is for another book), this is the first and only time so far that I have seen one. At no time did the snake even stop to look at me. It was on the move, doing its own business, as I was, and I didn't want to draw any attention to myself.

In September and October 2021, I had two encounters on my front patio. The first was at midnight. Archie wouldn't stop barking – one bark at a time, then a pause, then another bark. After lying in bed, yelling out to Archie to stop, but he wouldn't, I decided to get up, turn the patio light on and see what he was barking at.

Right outside my bedroom was a half-metre red belly black snake. It had reared up and Archie was at its tail, barking. I opened the door and called Archie inside. I went outside through the kitchen, grabbed a golf club, and saw that the snake had gone onto the deck behind a pot plant.

At that point, I knew I couldn't kill it. Not because I didn't know how, but because I just didn't want to. I tapped the golf club onto the deck, making vibrations to move it on. It started to move inside the pool fence, and I hoped that it didn't go into the pool, which it didn't. It moved towards the edge of the deck, fell off the edge and disappeared underneath – hopefully into the paddock.

I went inside and decided that Archie could sleep in my bedroom for the night. I didn't know if he had been bitten, so I stayed awake until 2 am to make sure he didn't have any side effects of a snake bite. Thankfully, he didn't, and the snake hasn't returned since.

What I realised was that during that day, I had cleaned out my woodshed 15 metres away from house. I probably disturbed the snake, and being the first warm night of spring, it came for a visit.

The next snake encounter was on the 15th of October 2021. I was on a video call with my family in Melbourne as it was my dad's birthday. Archie started to bark, and I knew instantly what was happening. I told my family I needed to go and check Archie and I would be back. To my amazement, I saw a small bandy-bandy snake on the patio near my bedroom.

Bandy-bandy snakes have a unique black-and-white-striped appearance. The snake I was looking at was only around 30-40 centimetres in length, and its back was arched above the ground like a rollercoaster. I called Archie inside immediately and went back to my family – I had to get my Steve Irwin gear on to tackle this snake!

Thankfully, I had a rake on the patio with a 1.8-metre handle and I put my gumboots on. I started to push the snake off the patio and towards my water tanks. I flicked it a couple of times towards the back of the house. It slipped under the fence and I flicked it a few more times before it went into the garden and started slithering towards the back paddock.

Another successful mission, and my family were happy to see me back safe and sound.

During November 2021, I had another two snake encounters. I have seen more snakes this year than the three years I have lived in Coolabine!

One was in the paddock when I was riding Minty. I had Archie and the other two horses with me in the back paddock. Archie alerted me by squatting down and moving around an object. As I got closer, being high up on Minty, I saw that it was a snake that had had a good feed and was basking in the sun. I called Archie off the snake, which he did, and we rode around it.

We had to ride past the snake on the way back to the house. I took the horses and Archie in a wide berth to avoid it. It was still in the paddock and, again, as I rode past, it didn't move. It looked like a very healthy tiger snake. I didn't stick around to take a photo; I just left it in the paddock to digest its meal and enjoy the sun.

The last sighting happened at 4 am in the morning. I was in bed asleep when Archie started barking. I yelled out to him and then realised it might be a snake. Sure enough, Archie was at the front gate watching a python slither across the driveway into the garden in front of the house. It was around one-and-a-half metres long and was moving slowly, as they do, slithering into the olive tree for some leisurely sightseeing.

Again, I called Archie off the gate, and he obeyed straight away. I didn't know whether the snake was going to come into the patio area, but at 4 am, I wasn't ready to tackle it. I took Archie into my bedroom, shut the doors and went to sleep.

I am very lucky that I can yell out 'off' to Archie and he will back away from the reptiles. He is a great guard dog and once I have come out to see what it is, he stops barking.

I share my property with all sorts of reptiles, foxes, and wild dogs. I have learnt over the last few years through videos, documentaries, and books that these animals don't want to attack you. Mostly they are on their way to a destination to eat and survive. I will avoid them at all costs and hopefully they will respect Archie and I and won't harm us in return.

My Lesson for You:

- If you are fearful of something, address it. Watching videos and educating myself on reptiles has enabled me to live with and respect them.
- Never approach a reptile. They are dangerous and a bite can be fatal.
- Don't run, scream or try to kill a reptile as you may come off second best. Educate yourself.
- Understand first aid. Knowing what I would need to do if I got bitten has helped me. When you live by yourself, there are a lot of times when you need to be self-sufficient.
- If you have a dog and live in the country, train them to move away from a reptile on command. Most dogs get bitten when the owner tries to save the dog.
- Reptiles are beautiful to watch, and they have a unique way of being calm, especially pythons.

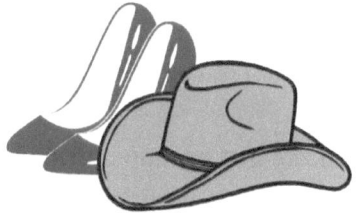

Chapter 13

Preparation for the Cabins Begins

I'm not entirely sure when my passion and dream of owning a bed and breakfast started. I just know it has been in my thoughts for the last 25 years.

As a child, I remember taking a trip from Mildura to Broken Hill. Halfway there, we stopped at a roadhouse. The lady behind the counter looked sullen and didn't seem like she wanted to be bothered by tourists. I wondered why she did a job that she hated. Was it the only way to pay the bills? Why couldn't she just move and do something else? I was only 12 at the time, so what did I know? But this stayed in my mind, and I never wanted to be that woman.

In 1998, Robert and I took a trip to the UK and Paris – our first trip together. For two weeks, we drove around England, Scotland and into Wales, staying at bed and breakfasts – a mixture of houses with amazing hosts. The hosts not only gave us beds for much more reasonable prices than a hotel, but they would give you their views on where and what to visit. I really loved the way they opened their homes and hearts to all who stayed there.

After we were married, we had a group of friends and all of us would go away with each year for two nights. Their kids would come too, and one of our favourite spots was in Healesville in Victoria. The property had three cabins, a one-bedroom and two two-bedrooms, built from wood and they had the feel of an old cabin.

Their property wasn't huge, but it was large enough to accommodate 10 adults and seven children. The fun we had at that place was memorable and inspired Robert and I that one day we would have a similar property of our own.

Over those years, and when we took girls' weekends away, we always hired a house or with cabins for our relaxation retreats. They were a time to get away and not have to go too far if we didn't want to. It always seemed to be in the winter months so a log fire was a must, and they were usually near country towns where we could go antique shopping and enjoy a taste of the local cafés.

After Robert relapsed in late 2017, he started to think about where he wanted to live and what he wanted the rest of his and our lives to look like. He didn't want to spend the rest of his working life in a corporate role, and if he had any chance of surviving this latest round of treatment and going into remission, removing all stress from his life would be necessary.

As I said previously, we started to look at properties in an around the Sunshine Coast Hinterlands. We found our new home and we moved in December 2018.

After April 2019, due to Robert's treatment and his deteriorating condition, we only got to go back to Coolabine twice before he died.

PREPARATION FOR THE CABINS BEGINS

In late May 2019, Robert had the opportunity to leave hospital and be treated as an outpatient. He had two weekends at home while we lived in Brisbane mid-week.

On the last weekend Robert was home, he had been in considerable pain and was going downhill. One morning he wanted to sit outside under our patio and have breakfast, looking up to the ridge and hills that were in front of our house.

I am not sure what Robert was thinking that day, but my parents, who were there, and I now reflect on that moment and think that, in some way, Robert may have been saying goodbye to Coolabine. Although he never gave up and always fought hard to conquer his illness, on this day there was something different, and, although it was hard on my parents and I, I was so happy that he was able to spend that weekend at home.

Two weeks later, and after being readmitted to hospital and transferred to palliative care, Robert lost his fight. He would never physically return to Coolabine. He would never see his dream of Coolabine Retreat being built. He would never welcome the guests that would stay in our retreat and enjoy a snippet of what I get to enjoy every day of living in the country.

After Robert died, I had a single-minded determination to fulfil our dream of building the business we had longed for – to welcome guests and give them a taste of country life, but more than anything, to see them leave our retreat more relaxed, happy and content than when they arrived.

Robert had given me the greatest gift of all, Coolabine Retreat. Although his intention was to build and grow our business together, he had the confidence that I could do this on my own. That I could fulfil the dream that we talked about for so many years. That I had the business acumen through my corporate role to run it successfully and escape the corporate life earlier than I ever imagined.

Three months after Robert had died, I made the decision to resign from corporate life – to step away from the job that I thought would fulfil me for at least another five years. The grief and pain that I had been through were starting to change my approach, tolerance and mindset, and I had made a promise not only to Robert at his bedside as he was dying, but to myself that I would make our dream a reality.

I was jobless, but I had a business plan, a spreadsheet and a vision. I didn't know how long it would take. I thought it would be a pretty easy process and once I was back in a more positive frame of mind and I was functioning more than grieving, I decided to start building this business.

PREPARATION FOR THE CABINS BEGINS

For months and months, I researched different kit homes, looking for a cheap way to build the cabins while still providing a different level of comfort and service to the Mary Valley. This wasn't working, as nothing seemed to really sit well with me.

I took my friend, Steve, to see one of the kit homes designs and although I was nearly sold on it, it still felt like a mining donger or a caravan cabin.

I then found a company in Gympie that offered designs that were closer to what I was looking for, but when I priced it up, it was going way above my initial budget. Again, I just didn't have that response in my gut that this was the one.

Then my friend, John, reminded me that a kilometre down the road from my house I had met a builder who said if I ever needed any work done to give him a call. I had met Mick only a few weeks after Robert had died. I was walking the dogs past his property as he was doing some excavating works to shift a Queenslander to this plot of land.

Mick seemed like a nice bloke. He had the skills and I had nothing to lose, so I rang him and asked him to drop by to look at my property and my potential business.

As soon as we walked out onto the ridge behind the house, he was in awe of the view. I took him through what I was looking at building. Starting with three cabins, possibly a pavilion and pool at a future stage and if everything was working out maybe glamping down in the gully.

He loved every piece of my vision and intention and said he would love to work with me on it. He told me that everything I had in mind for this business was what he would do. He loved the thought that we didn't have to disturb any flora, the uninterrupted views and concept of giving the cabins a luxury feel.

After our first meeting, he set me up with a draftsman who could design the cabin structures and set me on my way to building my dream.

The initial meeting and the follow-up meetings with the draftsman went well. All three of us were on the same page about the possibilities. The draftsman had also made the time to come out to my property to look at where the structures would sit. We talked about possibly constructing the maximum number of cabins the property could fit so that if I wanted to build more in future stages, I didn't have to go and get building approval for them.

From our discussions, everything seemed to be going great, until I started to hit some delays with the draftsman. At first, I gave him some space with the delays as he had some family issues that had seen him have to take unexpected time away from his business. But once that was over and he promised me dates of when the next version of the plans would be ready and he missed them twice, I started to get concerned.

What concerned me even more was that we were coming up to Christmas 2020 – we were in November, and I had engaged him back in August. I also didn't have a second version of the plans and he wouldn't return my calls. For three weeks I would call, text and email him to find out what was going on, but he wouldn't respond.

I was also ringing the builder who had referred him and started to ask him to intervene. Another two more weeks passed, and it was now the end of November. I gave the draftsman an ultimatum, saying that if he didn't want or have time to do my job, I would be happy for us to just go our separate ways. Mick the builder went and saw him

PREPARATION FOR THE CABINS BEGINS

for me, and he admitted he had taken on too much work. He was embarrassed about how he had treated me and he had to walk away.

Great, this wasn't the start I was wanting. I had to go back to the drawing board and start the process all over again. I didn't know who to engage; I was so frustrated that my dream that I thought was on track, really hadn't started at all.

As we went into December, I wondered if building this dream, by myself, was worth it. Did I really have the skills and patience to complete this project. Was I meant to run a business by myself?

What I did know was that I wasn't going back to corporate life. I wasn't going back to a job that I was working to make someone else rich. I had just written my first book and had engaged a publisher – I wasn't someone who gave up.

Yes, I had fallen off the horse, but I have more determination and resilience than most people I know. This was a road bump, maybe even a breakdown, but I had a builder who believed in me and my dream, and most of all, I believed in me!

It took a bit of soul-searching, but within a week, I was back on that horse, had engaged a new draftsman and started the plan to kickstart the process off all over again in January 2021.

2021 was going to be my year!

The year started off great with progress on the plans moving along well. I had engaged a town planner then needed to get a soil tester out to my property to assess whether the cabins could be built on the hill without falling and whether the grey water area and septic were able to be used.

Then the rain started. After two false starts, I finally got the soil tester out before Easter to do the assessments. He was a nice guy, but the guy with the machinery doing the digging was not and wouldn't listen to my guidance and didn't seem to want to talk to me.

I may not be too far out of Brisbane, but over the last two years I have come across a few men that don't want to liaise with me or don't acknowledge me when there are other males on site. In one case, they didn't even show up. I don't know how everything works in their world, especially their machines, but I worked in construction for several years and am always eager to listen and learn. If only some men were open to that.

It took a month for the soil plans to come back, having been delayed by three weeks. This was becoming a familiar occurrence and my patience, which isn't the greatest in any event, was starting to be tested. I just wanted to get the report, get the plans to the local council and get this show on the road. Did anyone else other than me get that?

After many delays and a few false starts, I finally had the final soil test report which was supportive of the build, the grey water and septic requirements. A final copy of the plans had been completed and in the third week of May 2021 the town planner confirmed we were going to go to the council. Woohoo!

Now, I had to play the waiting game to hear what the council would say. The average wait time for council approval is eight weeks, which would take me through to the end of July – for a project that I had planned to have already started building in June. I was at least four months behind that timeframe and started to worry when I would be earning an income again.

PREPARATION FOR THE CABINS BEGINS

Even after we submitted the rezoning plans to the council, we still had to get building approval and had to fit into the builder's schedule. The possibility of opening the cabins before Christmas felt like it was on a knife's edge. I just hoped the universe was going to be on my side!

In July 2021, I received the first response from the council. They had reported three items that they needed included or changed to continue the reassessment. The first one was to include more landscaping between the cabins. The second was to take pictures from each cabin site and show the outlook. The third item was that the two-bedroom cabins were too big.

The pictures of the view, which I assumed were to understand the outlook on to the neighbouring properties were minor. I had already told my neighbours about the cabins, so I didn't see any issues and they weren't close to me. Landscaping was easy as I was more than happy to plant more trees, plus the cabins are 50 metres apart so that was no bother. But the third one was concerning.

I knew when I submitted the plans to the council that there may have been some feedback about the size. But to reduce them by a third, which would mean only having one bedroom, was a shock. The council's reasoning is that the two bedrooms turned them into dwellings, that could be used to permanently house people and they were cracking down on these types of cabins. Whether it was my intention or not to use them for permanent rentals in the future, they didn't want any possibility of this happening.

Although I was disappointed with the response, the town planner told me that they hadn't said no and the adjustments were minor in the grand scheme of things. I could still ask for the cabins to be approved, the size adjusted and to move forward.

We adjusted the plans, taking off one bedroom and bathroom and reduced the size within the parameters of the council. As I talked to the draftsman, we decided that I could still have a sofa bed in the lounge room and design the open plan to have some sort of separation by putting in by fold doors etc. After some calm thinking, it all made sense and again I just had to remind myself that the plans will still going ahead and the council hadn't said no.

By the end of July, the second submission was back at the council and the clock was restarted again – so I had to sit tight for the next response!

I am learning to be more patient as I go through this process. I think because I am not working, although I am spending my time writing this book and even that feels hard to do, it is difficult for me to see the weeks go by and still be waiting on council's response.

I have had days where I have been depressed and didn't think I could build this dream. I have stopped looking at the business plan, numbers and stopped buying items for the cabins. I look at the 30 boxes of linen, towels and decorative pieces sitting in my entrance hall and wonder if I did the wrong thing by buying them. I just don't have the motivation to do any pre work while I wait for a response.

In late September 2021, the town planner gave us an update, telling us there was only the approval from the ecologist left to go. All other parties had approved it and it shouldn't take long to get this last one. With that in mind, I met up with the draftsman and finalised the internal plan of the cabins, the size of the pavilion and some other minor details.

Yay, we were back on the right path – things were moving again. We worked out that if all went to plan, we could aim for the building to

PREPARATION FOR THE CABINS BEGINS

start in mid-January 2022. I was happy with this on the knowledge I could get the business open by Easter 2022.

But as the weeks went by in October and the construction plans started to take shape, there had been no news from the council. I was again left feeling that our milestones were going to be missed again!

On the 22nd of October, I received the notification that the cabins had been approved. I still needed to get the report, but with minimal requirements, I was on the way now to opening our dream business.

The draft report came a week later, and whilst I was happy with most of the stipulations, a few concerned me. So, back to the council we went to get a few amendments. They came back and agreed with our changes, and by the first week in November, I had the approval.

I was able to build my short-term, 14-day accommodation business on my land where I wanted them. I then had to engage an engineer to create an operation works plan which would be submitted to Council. After that was approved, I could submit the building/construction plans and we could start building.

I now know that every step in this process has a delay. The engineering firm I engaged is inundated with work, like most on the Sunshine Coast, and won't be able to release their report until mid-January 2022. I will continue to work with the draftsman on the building plans and have them ready at the same time so we can submit them to council immediately after the operational plan is approved.

The January start date is long gone – we're now in April 2022. The engineer has finally undertaken a site visit and I am now waiting for his report.

The site visit, although it took a while, was well worth it. It enabled me to save around ten thousand dollars and I got the outcomes I wanted. Not a bad investment to have them on site for only an extra $400.

The final construction plans are ready to be submitted once I receive the engineer's report, but Covid and the February floods have disrupted the building industry tremendously.

Not only that, but build costs have increased by 40 per cent, and there is a risk of supply shortages for building materials. Although I want to open this business in August 2022, if it is open by Christmas, I will be happy.

I have been thrown lots of curveballs throughout this process, full of emotional ups and downs that nearly saw me pull the pin a few times.

But then I rethink what I want for the next 10 years. Fulfilling this dream, no matter what the delay or cost, is what I want to do. I keep making the phone calls and pushing all the people that matter to deliver my outcomes. I am determined to fulfil not only my own dream but to provide retreats that will help so many others to conquer their fears and move forward with their lives.

When I finally open these cabins, it will be a very special day!

My Lesson for You:

- When your gut says this doesn't feel right, act on it. If I had acted quicker to remove the work from the first draftsman, I would've been building my dream sooner.
- Continuously be on the back of the person that is holding you up. Get on the phone, ask them where they are up to, make sure you are pushing the project through.
- Work to the contingency timeline. I set an expectation within myself that it wasn't going to be delayed and continually disappointed myself.
- Believe in yourself and in your dream. I only ever doubted myself for around a week at each delay, but that meant I was down in the dumps for around a month in total. It didn't help the outcome, so I should've been kinder to myself.
- Never give up, never stop wanting to fulfil your dream. Get back on the horse as quick as you can and keep your energy high.

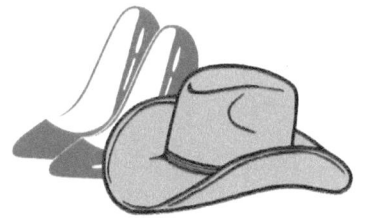

Chapter 14

Feeling Trapped

The Mary Valley where I live is home to the most picturesque valleys, waterways and quaint towns. From hiking to four-wheel driving, there are national parks, rivers and rainforests to enjoy.

That was one of the reasons Robert and I chose to look for a property in this area. We loved the fresh air, community feel and just having the country right on our doorstep.

When we inspected our property for the first time, the drive there allowed us to understand that this area, centred on the Mary River, was prone to flooding. My corporate role had involved managing flood events, and I knew this region had seen many floods, especially Gympie, which is 45 minutes from our place.

Between the nearest town Kenilworth and my home, there are nine floodway's. My neighbour who we purchased our house from told us that the waterfalls above and the creek systems flowed into the

Mary River. When the river rises, the water has nowhere to go, so flooding tends to happen for approximately twelve to 24 hours.

When we moved to Coolabine, we knew we always needed to have adequate supplies of food, torches, batteries, and access to a four-wheel drive to be able to live through such an event. After Robert's passing, I added solar energy to the house and battery backup so that I could still live and work if the power went out.

For the first two years of living alone at Coolabine, I experienced two rain events during which I was flooded in for 24 hours. I was able to cope with those, as I had all my supplies, power at the house through the batteries and enough food to last me at least two weeks.

Technology has made emergency flooding preparation a lot easier too. Most major rain events where you get more than 100 mm in a day are predicted days in advance by the Bureau of Metrology (BOM). I also follow Higgins Storm Chasing, an organisation which provides advice on what they expect from the BOM updates. Plus, my neighbours always update me and pre-warn me too, so I have always been prepared.

But what happened in February 2022 was totally unprecedented.

We had been warned that we may get up to 200 mm of rain for two days straight, then it would ease to 50 mm and disappear. Now that was a lot of rain, more than I had ever experienced. Because I was aware of this on 48 hours' notice, I went to my nearest town to buy extra groceries.

The rain began on the night of the 22nd of February and it woke me up with the noise on my tin roof. I let my dog, Archie, in, and allowed him to jump up on my bed to calm me. I was worried about my horses, hoping they would be protected by the trees in the paddock.

Archie laid beside me as I listened to the rain for a few hours before tiredness overcame me and I feel asleep.

When I woke up in the morning and looked outside my pool had overflowed, I could hear the water running through the creek below my house and the waterfall on the mountain on the ridge had formed.

I immediately went out to check on the horses and chickens. Both were high and dry, but I could see the water rushing out of the dam across the driveway, and the possibility of flooding was real.

Archie and I drove down to the front gate where we found the water was already over the second floodway, the creeks were high and the rain was persistent.

At this stage, the event was as predicted. We had had around 150 mm of rain up to 9 am. I took Archie into the paddock, where he ran in the creek, splashing and playing. He was having the best time; I loved watching him and I wasn't concerned for what may come next.

On the 24th of February, the rain was constant, and by the afternoon the weather system was right over the top of the valley and was at least 200km long and wasn't moving. There was no wind to move it and it kept circulating above.

I have experienced a few lows in Brisbane off the back of cyclones that hang over you for a few days, but nothing like this. We experienced another 200 mm that day, the rain did not stop, and I knew we would be flooded in.

Overnight, the rain was unrelenting. My sleep was interrupted all night. I continued to worry about the horses. I still had power which I was very grateful for. The scenes on the news, as I sat and watched them during the night, from the Government and the BOM, were that we were going to experience up to a year's worth of rain in this one period. That just seemed ridiculous to comprehend. I had 1300 mm of rain at my property last year, and they were saying we were possibly going to experience all of that in just one week.

In the morning, I spoke to my mum and told her that everything was ok. I thought we had had up to 600 mm so far, but I didn't know exactly as my solar rain gauge had stopped working due to no sun. The rain had eased in the morning, and it was just showers and I hadn't started to panic or worry about being flooded in.

But when I went out to check on the horses, the water crashing through my property, across my driveway and through my neighbour's paddocks was something I hadn't seen before. I was happy that the horses were on the house side of the creek and were safe but watching the water running across my easement which I share with my neighbour was like wild rapids. The sound from the waterfall was so loud, my creek through the gully was higher than I had ever experienced, and I started to feel uneasy.

As I watched and videoed the water running through and all around my property. my heart started to beat harder and harder. The magnitude and depth of the water started to mess with my mind and as I stood in the paddock, I began to have a panic attack.

I started to experience the feeling of being trapped. I walked around my house and onto the ridge. I knew my house wouldn't get flooded, but everywhere I looked, there was a torrent of water streaming all around me. It was like I had a giant moat around my house, and I knew that I couldn't get out.

I continued to watch until I felt like I couldn't breathe. I quickly walked back into my house and stood in the kitchen as the rain started to pound on the roof again. I started to feel nauseous and I was dry reaching over the sink. Through all my years of anxiety, I had never vomited. Now I was vomiting in the sink and my head was pounding. I went and sat on the couch attempting to do my meditative breathing exercises, but I couldn't control the anxiety that was rushing through my veins.

The devil in my head took full control of my mind, warning me that I was trapped. I couldn't get out, and if something happened to me, no one was coming to my rescue. I closed my eyes, trying to push the awful thoughts away, but they wouldn't stop. Tears were now forming in my eyes, rolling down my cheeks, and for the first time, I felt really scared.

I decided to do something that I would never recommend to anyone else, but at this moment in time I could think of nothing else to do. I poured myself a glass of wine and took three Panadol. I needed the thoughts, the anxiety, the physical shaking that was now moving through my body to stop. Medicating myself seemed like the only thing left to do.

As I waited for my heart to start to slow down, I took Archie in my arms and started to rock. I thought I was going out of my mind and the devil was telling me that if I had a heart attack or a stroke, no one was going to find me in time. That if I was able to ring 000 then how would they get to me. Would a helicopter land on my ridge and find me in time to save me?

I then didn't want to move in case I tripped over and knocked myself out. I was catastrophising every possible scenario and I couldn't stop it. As I finished the glass of wine and kept rocking on the couch, my eyes started to get heavy, and I somehow fell asleep. I don't remember how long I was asleep for, but when I woke up, I sat up quickly, grabbed my heart and realised I was alive.

All this happened over the space of two hours. From realizing I couldn't get out of my property, to waking up suddenly, wondering where I was and whether I was alive. I had come full circle through my anxiety attack. I continued to self-medicate and drink for the next couple of days. It wasn't what I should've been doing, but it eased the thoughts and anxiety to allow me to not do anything stupid to myself.

For the next two days, I sat in the house and regularly checked the horses through the day. The voices in my head continued and I received some calls from friends, but their support and care didn't seem to push my anxiety away. Sometimes, it made it worse.

I took videos and pictures of the water as it started to slow or recede. I had stopped watching the news as it made me even more anxious. Instead, I was watching live sport wherever I could find it on TV as it was the only thing I could concentrate on.

I couldn't read, I couldn't write, I couldn't seem to focus on anything but the weather and the only thing that was calming me down was wine and Panadol.

Thankfully on the 26th of February, I got a call from my neighbours saying they were coming up to see me, that the water over my driveway had dropped and they wanted to check in on me.

To be able to see them and talk about the events of the last four days was all that I needed. We worked out that we had had close to a metre of rain during those four days, something that my neighbour had never experienced before.

He had talked to a few neighbours, and everyone had fences down, gates down, or major flooding though their property. The floodway's were still overflowing, so we couldn't get into town. We saw photos on social media where bitumen roads had been washed away, tanks, large shipping containers had been washed down creeks and rivers and the weather system was now sitting over Brisbane.

Over the next 48 hours as the waters receded, I started to take charge of my anxiety. Knowing that within days that I could get out of my property was starting to have a positive effect on my thoughts. I wasn't drinking during the day, and I was able to start to focus on some hobbies that would allow me to calm down.

On Monday 28th February, I was able to drive into Kenilworth and see what the raging river system had done. So many farmers had lost fencing, their driveways and were already in their paddocks cleaning up.

FEELING TRAPPED

My damage was small compared to most, with a gate that needed replacing, a fence needing repairing and my roadway into my paddocks had been washed away. I also had minor flooding into my bedroom. The rain had been so heavy that when it hit my back wall of my bedroom, it had somehow seeped into my room, damaging my carpet, underlay and was now starting to smell.

I moved my bed into the middle of the room by myself, a feat in itself seeing it's a king-size bed. I lifted the carpet to reveal a wet underlay and put two fans pointing onto it to dry it out. I slept in my second bedroom while the carpet and underlay dried out and lodged an insurance claim that would see my carpet being replaced and wall repaired where the water had seeped in.

On the Tuesday, one week after the event had started the council was already out repairing the roads outside my property. Repairing a 1.5-metre sinkhole that had caused those residents on the south end of the road to not be able to drive to town. They started to repair the bitumen into town that had been swept into the paddocks, and the clean-up by the residents had begun.

The pictures in neighbouring towns were all over social media, including major flooding that had occurred in Gympie and Brisbane. The rain system was now making its way slowly down the east coast where Lismore, and many NSW towns had started to flood to unprecedented levels.

As I began to clean up around my house and property, I was so grateful for the wonderful community that I lived in, and that they were all coming to together to help each other and clean up the valley.

I then reflected on how I had responded and managed the event emotionally. I had all the materials and tools in place to physically get through a flood with food, batteries, torches and communications, but I hadn't realised the effect it would have on me mentally.

Although my methods through alcohol and medication were not what I would recommend to anyone to do ever, I managed myself enough to not allow it to harm me.

When I visited my counsellor two weeks later, we worked through the scenarios and she gave me a few extra tools and practices to use if my anxiety got to that extreme level again. I was very grateful that I had her there to help me through, and in hindsight I should have called her to help me when I was in those anxious moments.

When we bought our property in 2018, I had never expected such an event to happen, much less, ride out the storm by myself.

I knew my resilience, courage and strength was at a level that I could never have imagined. After going through this event in 2022 by myself, it had lifted to a whole new level.

I continue to come across new challenges as I move forward in my life. I never expected that at 49 I would be living and managing a 35-acre property by myself. I never imagined I would have to manage my emotional state by myself, but everything I am challenged with continues to be a new lesson that is stored in my memory.

I hope one day life gets a little easier, but I know all these events and lessons will come in good use one day and I have the confidence that I can concur anything by myself in the future.

My Lesson for You:

- Preparation before any weather or natural event is the key.
- Ensure you have an evacuation plan that you can execute.
- Your resilience will kick in when you let it.
- If you need to ring someone, especially mental health services then do so.
- The media can have a negative affect on your mental health so if images are worrying you, turn them off.
- Keep up to date with the right applications or social media sites that will help you.

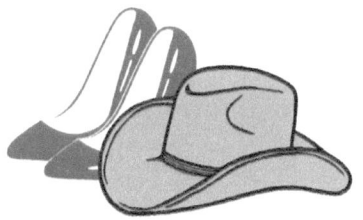

Chapter 15

Finding Me

For most of my corporate career as an executive, I felt like an imposter around my peers. I didn't have a bachelor-of-whatever degree or an MBA to hang on my wall. I had to reassure myself of my skills and capabilities, which was hard. I had to remind myself that when I had been promoted and taken on that next business unit, it was because of my track record to get results, not because I had an IQ like the guy sitting next to me.

So many times, I would shut the door to my office or go for a walk and my head kept saying that I wasn't good enough, wondering if they would get rid of me because I was not smart enough. At night I would lay in bed asking myself, 'Can I do this? Can I have this conversation tomorrow? Can I say what I need to say at that meeting? Can I stand up and address the room?'

Looking back now, I was uncomfortable at least once a day, and I don't know how I did it. I continually doubted and compared myself to others, but I also continually fought for myself – who I was, my brand, what I stood for. I may not have been the smartest in the room, but I got shit done and that's what got me through most days. My resilience and track record shone through. Most of the time, my team worked hard for me, which gave me the confidence to get out of bed and do it all again the next morning.

If I had to do something at work that I didn't know how to do, I would google how others did it, buy their book and watch their videos. I would spend countless hours researching so I had the confidence to execute it. Because I didn't have a certificate on the wall, I learnt as I went. I upskilled myself on what I needed to execute, and I copied what was successful for others.

I still do the same today, but I don't have the angst that used to come with it. If I need to buy a new tool and don't know how to use it, I read the instructions. If I need to change the chain on the chainsaw, I get the manual out and do it. I don't procrastinate on what is the best way because if I don't have the manual, I google it.

When I use a tool for the first time, I don't get worried about what others will think about me. When I walk the paddocks spraying the weeds, the only thing I worry about is keeping myself safe. I don't have anyone telling me I missed a spot or didn't spray it properly! What a change from a world where I felt like a lot of people were looking over my shoulder, criticising me for what I had or hadn't done, rather than patting me on the back and saying well done.

Reflecting on this now, I know they weren't my tribe. The corporate world was not what I was destined to be part of. Was I faking it? No way. I worked damn hard, probably harder than some, to get the outcomes, results and skills to do the roles that I did. What made it hard was being on my own. At times, people didn't want to help you.

They couldn't wait for you to fall on your sword and were happy to swoop in behind you and take the glory.

Being in the country, living and owning 35 acres, you are your own boss. When you do ask for help, it is forthcoming. No one criticises you for asking for help. No one criticises you when you ask how to do things, because you have never done it before. No one stands behind you, waiting for you to fail. The generosity, the helping hand, the support to want you to succeed is endless out here.

It has taken me so long to be comfortable in my own skin. When I worked in corporate, I was always worried about how I looked, what I wore, how I conducted myself. My wardrobe was full of so many clothes for work. The jackets, suits, blouses and shoes. OMG, the shoes; it was out of control. I look back now and my husband was right: I didn't need that top in three different colours. But I had this saying that you need to look like you can do the job, even if you doubt yourself.

When I saw a photo of myself at work and I didn't think I looked right, I would stop wearing that piece of clothing. If I went to a conference, which we did at least four times a year, I made sure I had a new outfit. I didn't want to be seen in the same attire that I wore last time. This was extreme in so many ways. The guys I worked with didn't care what I wore, but I did. I had to stand in front of the mirror before I left the house or hotel and know that I could fit in in a material sense!

What a change it has been for me. Going from the corporate suits, makeup and groomed hair to a casual, carefree country lifestyle. Today, I feel more comfortable than ever. I love putting on my jeans, shorts or jodhpurs to go into the paddocks. I love my polo tops, work shirts and faded, paint-splattered, dirt-covered t-shirts. I love my caps and Akubra that shield me from the sun and hide my dirty hair, especially when it hasn't been washed for days!

I have found my place, I have found my uniform, I have found me! What I wear today is so much more comfortable and suits who I am. I am not being fake, I am not trying to match it with the boys, I am not trying to compete with the girls, with the people that don't mean anything to me. I am only out in the paddocks being my authentic self to help myself – me, myself, no one else.

I am discovering the more that I live this life that I have used several skills that I learnt in the corporate world to get to where I am today. To build my cabins, I need to project manage them and influence people to deliver the outcomes I need. I have written published my first book, which has come from the report writing skills, the speeches and the many emails I have had to write over that time.

Hosting and speaking at corporate events have enabled me to talk in front of groups about my book, do interviews and introduce myself to key groups. Driving long distances by myself, especially between home and Brisbane, was a practice I had to do when I led the Queensland teams and I know how to occupy myself.

There are so many skills beyond these that I leverage every day. But the biggest lesson I have learned is giving it a go. Every failure or false start brings you closer to success. That nothing is too hard to learn if you have the mental strength and passion to do it. Never doubt how strong you are. You are only as strong as you need to be and sometimes that strength is hidden until you need it.

In 2020, I decided that I needed to join a few groups that would allow me to meet likeminded women. That would inspire me to be my best self and start to build new networks. Networks that were outside the corporate world I had been in, that were local and with women who had built their own small businesses.

I joined the Women's Business Network on the Sunshine Coast. The first event I went to was just before Christmas in 2020. I dressed up in a summer dress with heels that I ended up getting blisters from as I hadn't worn them in so long. I went by myself and within minutes of arriving, three other women who had also come by themselves joined me. It was nice to meet women who were also out of their comfort zone attending the event by themselves.

After the initial event, I attended a few other breakfasts. I found that I was starting to become more introverted around these women, not wanting to mingle, not wanting to share my own story as I felt that I didn't fit in. Now, I am not saying that these women were fake or not nice to be around, but I didn't feel comfortable in the environment because to me, attending these functions took me right back to my corporate world. That was a world where I didn't feel like I fit in, that everyone was looking at the new girl who didn't belong to the club.

I know that it was me who had the issue, not them. Every function I went to was wonderful. I heard from some great speakers, some inspirational stories and met some very hard-working and successful women. But the groups during this time weren't for me. I felt that I needed to establish my business and have something more meaningful before I could start attending their functions again.

The group I have found most interesting to be part of is the publishing group through which I wrote my first book. I have met several women who inspire me, who speak my language, who are out there to help others to be part of something that is bigger than themselves and to celebrate life.

I listen to several of their interviews and podcasts. I love watching them grow and extend their footprint beyond their family and friends. No one is criticised, no one is watching from the sidelines waiting for them to fail; they are all there to help, support and offer gratitude.

I watched one of these women launch her second book. She talked about how she didn't feel comfortable in her executive role, that she wanted to do more for others and that writing a book gave her the avenue to grow her new life.

I also loved that she sat on her live event in her gym gear and puffy jacket. There was no makeup, no script and her words were raw and from the heart. She told us that she can't spell properly, that she isn't perfect, and neither is her book. But she is manifesting a life and a world that will benefit herself, her family and so many others. It was inspiring to watch and listen and I felt that this is the tribe, my group, the people that I want to be around.

In 2022, I will be volunteering once a week with an organisation called Raise. I will undertake a 22-week mentoring program through a local high school with a teenager that needs support beyond school and family. I can't wait to provide support and be a role model who will inspire and help a young person to one day fulfil their dream because they met me.

I will continue to support my godchildren, my nieces, nephews and any child or adult that I can motivate and inspire. I feel that I have so much to give to this world to the people who want me in their world. I love seeing others smile and prosper because of who I am now. I have never had such confidence in myself, and the loving people around me are supporting my growth.

This is why I know I am now in the world I was meant to be in. I am now starting to grow into the person I want to be. I am more comfortable in my own skin. I love myself whenever I look in the mirror and don't have to put the suit and makeup on to show up every day. I don't doubt myself on my property, I only prosper. Those that have stuck with me on this journey are watching me grow. I have never felt as whole as I do today.

I forgive all the haters, devils and egos for showing me that I never want to be like you. Thank you for pushing me to the point that made me stronger, who made me more resilient and made me realise that I was always a better person than you. You may have dinted my soul when I worked with you, but I have come out stronger than ever.

I can't shy away from the fact that sometimes you must go through the hard times to learn the lessons and take strength from those experiences to know who you are and what you want to be. It's hard to rationalise life sometimes, but if you are a good person, you will know it, because there are more people on your side than not.

For every little girl or boy out there – every mother who wants their daughters or sons to be proud of who they are and what they want to be in life, this is for you. May my book bring you inspiration, may you never give up, may you ride out the bad times and use your experiences as lessons. May you always be true to yourself, trust your gut instinct and find a way to love yourself more than anyone else. May you be proud of what you do and how you do it and never let anyone get in the way of fulfilling your dream.

When I was little, I was the shy girl, but when I put on a costume and went on stage to dance, my true personality shone through. Don't wait for the costume – dance in the rain, splash in the ocean, take that hike, holiday or risk if that is what your instinct is telling you and remember to always be your authentic self.

I know Robert is staring from above and watching me grow as an individual. He would be telling everyone up there, 'That's my girl. I'm so proud of her. Never stop believing in you!'

My growth and future look so wonderful. I have so much still to give, so much to write, so much to fulfil. My heart has become fuller during 2022 than I ever thought was possible. The universe is sending the people I need in my life and I can't wait to write the next chapter and next book on how I became so much fuller on the back of my challenges and adversity.

Dreams do come true – look at me!

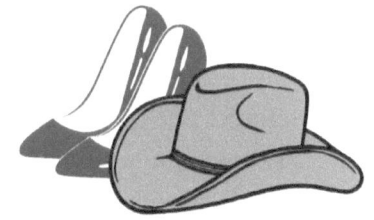

Acknowledgements

Writing my second book was easy at first. The words rolled off my fingertips and onto the pages for the first month until, bang, it stopped. I couldn't express my feelings, I sat down at the laptop and what was coming out was not what I wanted to say, and I just felt blah.

It took me four months with the help of my counsellor to understand what was blocking me, why I couldn't write and how was I going to get out of this rut. I had spoken to friends who are so eager to read this book, but I felt overcome by fear and just couldn't seem to shift it.

It wasn't until I watched another author promoting their second book via live video that I felt motivated again. She also spoke about her inability to write at times, that she had been through moments when she couldn't get the words out. Writing is not an easy process, but I knew that there was a story to tell. Not a story for me, as I already know it, I've lived it, but a story for others to be inspired by, to question their own life and gain the strength to fulfil their dreams.

The first person I want acknowledge is Robert. Beyond my parents, he was the one person who always made me try things when I didn't think I could do it. He was my number one supporter when I was climbing up the corporate ladder. He made me realise what was important in life and whatever we did, he always made it fun.

Although he isn't here with me now, I draw on his fight, strength, authenticity and humour every day. I know I wouldn't have been able to achieve all of this if I hadn't met and married Robert. I am so proud of who I am and who we were together, and I know he is walking beside me every step of the way.

Next are my parents. Since I was a young girl, you supported everything I did, what I achieved and celebrated my successes. You picked me up when I was down, you disciplined me when I did wrong and you have cared for and helped me beyond what I ever expected when Robert died. I now know that all my childhood lessons were worth it. Being taught wrong from right, good from bad, has held me in good stead for this life. I love you both beyond words. You are my number one supporters and I am proud to call you my parents.

John and Di, you have been such supportive friends over the 22 years I have known you, but I am even more appreciative of what you do for me today and the fun we have doing it. I have learnt so many skills from you John and I hope I have been a great apprentice. My property wouldn't be looking as good as it does, if I didn't have you helping me. Di, you are not only my cook and cleaner when you visit, but you are my friend and confidante. We have shared so much over the last few years and I love having you in my life.

Steve, my mate, you have been my amazing tradie. We haven't always built things the most conventional way, we have surprised ourselves a few times, but you never complain about how hard it is digging

ACKNOWLEDGEMENTS

holes, or what the weather's like, and we have schemed up so many damn businesses whilst building together that we really should be millionaires by now. But most of all, you are my mate and I have so much appreciation for you taking the time out and supporting my dream.

Daryll and Ally, my Queensland parents, I am so grateful that you made the decision to move back to Queensland and be part of my life in Coolabine. You are not only great house sitters, but you are wonderful friends. Daryll, you have completed some amazing projects for me. No one has a tool shadow board like me. You have made all my male friends extremely jealous. Ally, you have cooked and cleaned the house and loved my chickens more than me – and your blower vac skills are tops! Thanks for caring for the animals as much as I do; they love your visits, but I love having you visit even more.

I can't thank Ally enough for taking the photo that has created my amazing book cover. A photo that at first was going to be the draft cover, has now become part of my marketing material. Thank you so much for always capturing the beauty of Coolabine Retreat.

My gorgeous friends, Kyran and Mitch. You are always there for me when life hasn't gone my way. You have helped me to see the light, you have continued to love and care for me and have always been by my side. I love you both so much – our weekends at Coolabine, my weekends at your place, my ability to say whatever I feel and your honesty to steer me in the right direction are priceless. You are my friends for life.

To everyone who has been there for me through good times and bad, you have celebrated the achievements, given me the confidence to keep going and give it another go and you have patted me on the back and hugged me when I've cried. You are the most amazing friends in the world and I wouldn't want to live life without any of you.

Then there is me. When I took on the opportunity to write this book, I knew I was going to go back into the archives and drag out some memories that I wanted to leave in the past. Some of them will be buried again, some of them will be taken forth as part of who I am and the woman I will be.

My life is taking such a positive path, and I love the new people who have recently started walking alongside me. I continue to learn, love and be a better person than I ever thought I could be. I am already thinking about my next book and what I can continue to offer to those who look to me for inspiration and motivation.

I will always be grateful for every experience I have gone through. I am so proud of what I have achieved. I am so proud to be a role model to the next generation. I am so proud of ME!

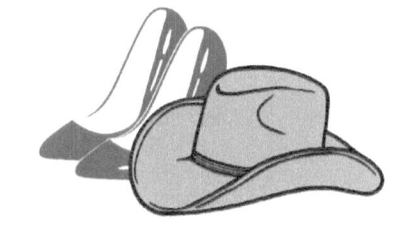

About The Author

Suzanne was born in 1973 to loving parents, Noel and Pat, and grew up in the Western Suburbs of Melbourne with her brother, Paul. Always a good student, Suzanne loved dancing, reading and going on holidays with her family.

After studying nursing at university, Suzanne instead found herself navigating a corporate career, from call centre consultant to successful executive.

Suzanne never set out to be an executive, but she strived to be the best she could in every role. This led her to be noticed by many in the organisation as she had a passion for people and enjoyed leading large teams.

After marrying Robert in 1999 and moving to Queensland in 2009, they lived a wonderful and happy life until Robert was diagnosed with leukaemia in 2013. From here, he endured six years of treatment and relapses, whilst Suzanne juggled being his carer and a corporate executive, before Robert eventually lost his fight in June 2019.

In 2018, the couple had moved to Coolabine, two hours north of Brisbane, on a 35-acre property to live out their dream of building an accommodation business catering to short term guests and to running group retreats.

After Robert passed, the dream was up to Suzanne. With the resilience, courage, and determination that she has built throughout her corporate and personal life, their dream is now her reality.

Suzanne published her first book *From Wife to Widow* in 2021 and has helped many who have gone through loss and life after. She volunteers at a nearby high school through the organisation Raise while also managing Coolabine Retreat.

She also loves to spend time with her dog, Archie, her three horses, friends, and family. Her life has been a rollercoaster of emotions, although she is a true believer that you can achieve anything if you put your mind to it.

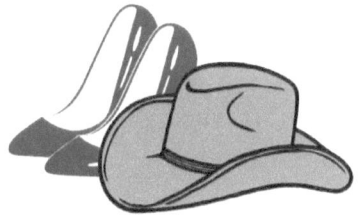

From Corporate to Country
Bonus Offer

Career Plan Framework

During my 25-year corporate career, I was grateful to have many managers who assisted in my development.

Unfortunately, not everyone has that support. Businesses don't facilitate employee/manager meetings, and without these frameworks, we begin to question why we aren't being considered for or winning that next role.

Through my experience as a leader, coach and mentor, I have learnt that you need to have a career plan that you will develop over a five-to-ten-year period to set you for success.

I have developed a framework that will enable you to put a plan in place to build your skills and drive. It will give you the questions that I needed to consider that enabled me to win my dream corporate role.

New Business Framework

Not knowing where to start when you are contemplating opening your first business can be daunting.

The statistics on failed businesses can often leave doubt in your mind about whether you want to join them, or if you want to thrive in business instead.

Many people who start their own business and fail haven't done the due diligence and planning before they jump in.

While I was working in my executive role, I began to develop my business plan, which gave me the insight and confidence I needed to open my new business.

My framework will provide you with questions that you may or may not have considered before launching into a new business.

This is not everything you need to put in place, and many more comprehensive templates can be found online, but this template will enable you to start compiling your thoughts and considerations and take action to be able to launch your new business!

Download your free copy of the Career Plan or New Business Framework at www.suzannegomes.com.au/ebook

Suzanne Gomes

Before becoming a small business owner, **Suzanne Gomes** was a corporate executive in one of Australia's iconic companies for over 25 years, leading large teams and speaking and chairing major events.

From her humble start in a call centre, to leading teams of thousands, to being a manager in a male-dominated industry, Suzanne has always made a real impact. Her career has not only been full of amazing achievements, but many challenges along the way.

Suzanne's life was turned upside down when her husband, Robert, was diagnosed with leukaemia that got the better of him six years later when he passed away in June 2019.

Suzanne's determination, strength and resilience have led her to be a corporate executive, her husband's carer, and now widow – and nothing could stop her from building her dream.

When it came to the decision of staying comfortable in her corporate role or diving into the world of small business, she chose the latter. She put the heels and city life behind her and decided to build her dream accommodation business in the Sunshine Coast Hinterlands in Queensland.

Suzanne has an incredible thirst for inspiring people of all ages, and knows what it takes to love and be kind to herself. She has been able to continuously grow and has found her purpose in life.

Suzanne is available to speak to support groups and organisations on:

Building a career
- Being the best version of yourself
- Saying yes to that next role
- Having a mentor and sponsors

Building Resilience
- How to say no
- Trusting your gut and intuition
- Speaking up when you're not being heard

Following your dream
- Finding your passion
- Building a plan
- Being true to yourself

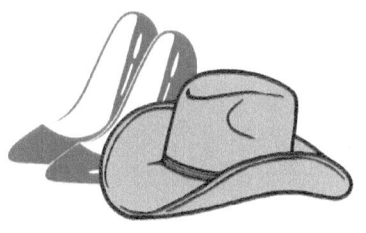

Notes

NOTES

NOTES

NOTES

www.ingramcontent.com/pod-product-compliance
Lightning Source LLC
Chambersburg PA
CBHW021433080526
44588CB00009B/518